People

CELEBRITY PUZZLER
SUPERSTARS

CONTENTS

PAGE 76

PAGE 12

WELCOME
TO *PEOPLE'S*
Celebrity Puzzler: Superstars!

- -

People is known for its addictive game collections,
highlighting your favorite celebrities. In this superstar-packed
edition you'll find the classic crosswords,
word searches and Second Look spot-the-difference
challenges. Whodoku puzzles, criss-crosses and arrow-words
are here too. On your mark . . . get set . . . Puzzle!

Puzzler on TV!

The Game Show Network series *People Puzzler* should look a little familiar to the magazine's regular crossword solvers. Based on the popular print game, the show is hosted by Leah Remini

Here's a riddle: How can you enjoy a crossword puzzle without ever lifting a pen or a pencil?

By watching People Puzzler, *on Game Show Network. Hosted by Emmy-winning producer and actress Leah Remini, the show, which airs Monday through Friday, puts three contestants' pop culture knowledge to the test as they attempt to complete sets of crossword puzzles. The player who earns the most points after three rounds gets the chance to play for a cash prize of up to $10,000. People spoke with Remini about her love of puzzles, and her TV quizmaster gig.*

On the show, contestants race to see who knows more about pop culture and complete a series of crossword puzzles.

It was coming from an authentic place of loving to try to solve the puzzle. I also love engaging with real people as opposed to a celebrity-based show. And I get to give people money! How fun is that? As we do the show, I am learning that I wouldn't do well as a contestant! This game is really set up for the players to win. Not only do the contestants get letters on the board to get them going, they also get a clue… and I still don't know the answers! I would be the contestant saying, "Yeah, I have no clue what that is still; I'm just going to go home"… and there's like one letter missing in the word. I don't do well when a timer is involved. So I have literally jumped up and down when they get it right! The people who do these shows are truly happy to be there. I love their excitement!

What makes a great game-show host?
I think what I liked about the game shows I grew up with as a kid was the host's connection with the contestants. You felt like the host was always on the side of the contestant and wanted them to win! And I think because of that connection, the contestants felt more at ease, had fun and felt someone was on their side under extreme pressure. And I hope to bring that to the contestants of *People Puzzler*. I am preparing by attempting to listen to my husband's stories about sports and golf and pretending to be interested.

Where do you get your crossword fix— and are you an ink or pencil person? What's your strategy?
Now, I want you to know, I'm not just saying this because it's you guys: I am a fan of *People*'s crossword puzzle because I can attempt to do them without feeling stupid. Always in pencil. I'm not that confident to do it in pen. I also have a crossword puzzle game on my phone called Wordscapes. My strategy is, I go for the ones I know first and focus on getting the words that connect. In that game there is an option for clues as far as letters, and I never use them. I really try to do the puzzle myself. Or I will randomly ask people by showing them my phone and say, "What do you think this word

is?" So, I do cheat and then lie to myself that I solved the puzzle myself.

Have you ever been doing a puzzle and seen your own name as a clue or answer?
Yes! It's been in *People*! I always send it to my mom when I am in the puzzle with a text: "Look, Ma, I made it."

What game shows did you grow up on?
I loved game shows as a kid! Now I'm really dating myself here. But I loved *The Price Is Right, Password, The Dating Game, The Newlywed Game, The Gong Show, Family Feud* and *Hollywood Squares.*

What appealed to you about *People Puzzler* as a show to host?

What is the best thing about it?
I can tell you that I haven't had this much fun in a long time. Because 2020 [was] a tough year emotionally, experiences like this of getting back to work have been a gift. The game is fun, and what I've been told over and over again from our producers is that they just want people at home to have a good time, and I love that message. •

CROSSWORD

Back by popular demand, it's Puzzler, the crossword compendium of popular-culture superstars. There's the blockbuster movie stars you'd expect (Jennifer Lawrence, Dwayne "the Rock" Johnson, Chris Pratt), joined by sensational musical artists (Lady Gaga, Cher, Jay-Z) and more. So turn the page—it's crowded in here.

21 ACROSS

Galaxy Star

ACROSS

1 ___ Worthington (*Avatar* costar of 21 Across)
4 Tracy Morgan comedy ___ *Out*
7 Arkin or Alda
11 21 Across's *Blood Ties* costar Clive ___
13 *Selma* and *13th* director Duvernay
14 ___ *of the Planet of the Apes*
15 Reality star Leakes
16 Celebrity cook Rachael ___
17 *Resident* ___: *The Final Chapter*
18 Author Umberto ___
20 Shaquille ___
21 A *Guardians of the Galaxy* star (2 wds.)
26 Eckhart or Paul
27 ___ Miss (University of Mississippi nickname)
28 Martin Freeman's *A World's* ___
31 Take it on the ___ (suffer defeat)
32 ___ and outs
33 Sam Shepard play ___ *of the Mind* (2 wds.)
34 Chad Michael Murray of ___ *Records*
35 Kurosawa film classic
36 Ichabod ___ (Johnny Depp's *Sleepy Hollow* role)
37 Creator-star of *Girls* (2 wds.)
39 Take ___ off one's feet (2 wds.)
42 Japan's former prime minister Shinzo ___
43 21 Across miniseries *Rosemary's* ___
44 Disney's ___ *and Maddie*
46 ___ the line (followed rules)
50 End in ___ (be even; 2 wds.)
51 Country music's ___ Young Band
52 *One* ___ *Hill*
53 *The* ___ *Hunter*
54 "The Big Easy" of golf, Ernie ___
55 TV's ___ *You the One?*

DOWN

1 ___ *of Zorn*
2 Shock and ___
3 *X-*___: *Apocalypse*
4 Comedy great Burnett
5 Egg cells
6 ___ *It Forward*
7 Madison Square Garden, e.g.
8 ___ *by Night* costars 21 Across
9 ___ Kate Dillon of *Billions*
10 *The Rocky Horror Picture Show's* Campbell
12 Actor Liam ___
19 *Kevin* ___ *Wait*
20 *The* ___ stars Jet Li
21 Efron and Posen
22 Jack Johnson's Hawaiian birthplace
23 *Dancing with the Stars'* Andrews
24 Designer Karan
25 Pacino and Martino
28 *In the Valley of* ___
29 Singer Simone's biopic starring 21 Across
30 Judge; reckon
32 McShane of *John Wick: Chapter 2*
33 Will ___ of *The LEGO Batman Movie*
35 Chris Hemsworth's ___ *Dawn*
36 Chicago team member
37 ___ *Cake* with Daniel Craig
38 Bette, Geena or Viola
39 Bon Jovi's "You Give Love ___ Name" (2 wds.)
40 ___ *Night* with Seth Meyers
41 Off-Broadway award
44 Jonny ___ Miller
45 "___ Be There"
47 "Poison" by Rita ___
48 Always, to Christopher Marlowe
49 Sandra or Kiki

Answers on page **118**

15 ACROSS

Chart Topper

ACROSS

1 "___ It Rain" (15 Across song)
5 Sound booster at a concert
8 ___-Wan Kenobi
11 "Single Ladies (Put a Ring ___)" (2 wds.)
12 "___ House" (15 Across song)
14 The ___ Pack (Sinatra and friends)
15 English pop star (2 wds.)
17 42 Across's network
18 Part of *SNL* (abbr.)
19 25 Down's Dr. ___
20 "___ thirsty, my friends"
22 Be a couch potato
23 *Mayberry R.F.D.*'s Aunt ___
24 "___ of You" (song performed by 15 Across at the 2017 Grammys)
27 "Thinking ___"

(15 Across's Grammy-winning song in 2016; 2 wds.)
31 Daytime host Kelly ___
32 2012 Taylor Swift album featuring 15 Across
33 Moon goddess
34 Phil or Ronnie ___ of early rock and roll
36 ___ of Endearment
37 Have a meal
38 Berlin's country (abbr.)
39 *Airplane!* star Robert ___
41 Rockwell or Waterston
42 ___ *Brother* (reality show hosted by Julie Chen)
45 *CSI* character played by William Petersen
46 "I Kissed a Girl" singer (2 wds.)
49 Grand ___ Opry
50 *Better Call* ___
51 "The A ___" (15 Across's first big hit)
52 *Sister Wives* network
53 "Honest ___" Lincoln
54 Mama ___ Elliot

DOWN

1 Homer Simpson's watering hole
2 *Four Weddings ___ Funeral* (2 wds.)
3 Star-___ tuna
4 Number suffix
5 Wide awake
6 Insignificant
7 Golf organization (abbr.)
8 *Free Willy* whale
9 *Bridget Jones's ___* (2016 comedy in which 15 Across had a cameo)
10 ___ *Complicated* (Meryl Streep movie)
13 First stage
16 Actress Falco
21 Penn & ___
22 Out of touch with reality
23 *Harold and Maude* star Cort
24 12th graders (abbr.)
25 ___-hop, a.k.a. rap
26 *Tarzan the ___ Man*
27 "___ the ramparts we watched . . ."
28 Young-adult-book-turned-movie *The Fault in ___ Stars*
29 Albuquerque school (abbr.)
30 ___ *Boot* (World War II movie)
32 Zombie condition
35 Jobs on a to-do list
36 Office worker for the day
38 Oprah's pal King
39 "Castle on the ___" (15 Across song)
40 Baldwin or Guinness
41 Piece of a theater ticket
42 La ___ Tar Pits
43 Gershwin and Levin
44 Workout settings or space
45 *You've ___ Mail* (Tom Hanks and Meg Ryan classic)
47 Auto club initials
48 "Yadda, yadda, yadda . . ."

24 ACROSS

Funny Favorite

1	**2**	**3**	**4**	▓	**5**	**6**	**7**	**8**	▓	**9**	**10**	**11**
12				▓	**13**				▓	**14**		
15				**16**					**17**			
▓	▓		**18**			▓	**19**					
	20	**21**			▓	**22**	**23**				▓	▓
24				▓	**25**				▓	**26**	**27**	**28**	**29**
30			▓	**31**			▓	**32**		**33**		
34			**35**		▓	**36**			**37**			
▓		**38**	**39**			▓	**40**				▓	▓
41	**42**	**43**			▓	**44**			▓	▓		
45			▓	**46**	**47**			▓	**48**	**49**	**50**	
51			▓	**52**			▓	**53**				
54			▓	**55**			▓	**56**				

ACROSS

1 *Sinbad: Legend of the Seven* ___
5 Slightly open, as a door
9 Antipollution org. in *The Simpsons Movie*
12 *Hawaii Five-0* island
13 Timber wolf, or a '70s and '80s TV sheriff
14 Onetime NBC slogan: Must-___ TV
15 2011 Sexiest Man Alive who's costarred with 24/36 Across in *Serena* (2 wds.)
18 Hair coloring
19 Johnny Depp's *Lone Ranger* role
20 Max ___ Jr. (Jethro in *The Beverly Hillbillies*)
22 *The Incredibles* boy with a speedy name
24 With 36 Across, *The Hunger Games* star
26 *X-Men* creator Lee
30 Suffix with hallow on Oct. 31
31 Hot chocolate
33 Adams who costarred in *American Hustle* with 24/36 Across
34 RuPaul's ___ *Race*
36 See 24 Across
38 Giuliani of New York City
40 Former senator Feingold
41 Ayn Rand's ___ *Shrugged*
44 Great Lake ending after Super
45 He played Gale in *The Hunger Games* alongside 24/36 Across (2 wds.)
51 *Pirates of the Caribbean: At World's* ___
52 U2's "___ Better Than the Real Thing"
53 *Au* ___ (1999 Fox Family TV movie)
54 Scoundrel
55 Move, in Realtor-speak
56 24/36 Across's are blue

DOWN

1 Cry out loud
2 Pointy one for Spock
3 "So that's it!"
4 ___ *Impact* (*Dirty Harry* film)
5 Away from the wind, aboard the *Bounty*
6 Miracle Mop film for 24/36 Across
7 *Jimmy Kimmel Live!* network
8 1977 or 2016 Kunta Kinte miniseries
9 SportsCenter network
10 *Togetherness* actress Amanda ___
11 ___smith, Steven Tyler's band
16 "He's a real nowhere man," e.g.
17 Reacts to fireworks
20 Sudsy drink for Norm in *Cheers*
21 Paquin in *X-Men: Days of Future Past* with 24/36 Across
22 Tooth damage
23 Get one's ducks in ___ (2 wds.)
24 President's first name on *The West Wing*
25 Drop out, in poker
27 Catches some rays
28 Some movie theaters
29 Bill ___ the Science Guy
32 Feathered weapon for Katniss Everdeen
35 Metric fat unit
37 Continent where *Gladiator* is set
39 "My Boo" singer
41 Baldwin or Guinness
42 Fey of *30 Rock*
43 Diane or Cheryl ___
44 "Money ___ object" (2 wds.)
46 Adam and ___
47 Gibson in *The Beaver* with 24/36 Across
48 Billy ___ Cyrus
49 Justin Timberlake's "Suit & ___"
50 *48* ___ (Nolte-Murphy action comedy)

Answers on page **118**

23 ACROSS

Ultimate Athlete

ACROSS

1 ___ *Gyver* (revived TV series)
4 Bestselling author Child
7 *Last ___ Standing* with Tim Allen
10 Prince Aly Khan's dad
11 ___ *Breathe* with Stephen Lang
12 ___s Peak
13 Middle "S" in S.S.S., for short
14 *Bridge of Spies* features Alan ___
15 "I Am Not My Hair" by India.___
16 First name of 23 Across
18 *X-Men: The Last ___*
19 "___ on a Grecian Urn"
20 Commentator-author Buchanan
21 The Beatles' "I Want to ___ Your Hand"
23 Tennis superstar (with 16 Across)
28 Pooh's erudite friend
29 Tennis-pro sister of

23 Across (first name)
30 Skater Babilonia
31 *Django Unchained* and *Appaloosa*, e.g.
33 *Hawaii Five-0* star O'Loughlin
34 ___-i-o ("Old MacDonald" refrain)
35 "Body on Me" singer Rita ___
36 Number of Wimbledon titles 23 Across has earned
39 Marvel's ___ *of S.H.I.E.L.D.*
42 23 Across won the US ___ six times
43 Israel's Golda ___
45 "You're Nobody ___ Somebody Loves You"
46 *Grand Ole ___*
47 ___ *and Seek* with Robert De Niro
48 Food Network's Garten
49 National Security Agency (inits.)
50 *Notes ___ Scandal* (2 wds.)
51 Waterston or Worthington

DOWN

1 *Black ___* with Johnny Depp
2 Author-critic James ___
3 Diahann, Jim and Lewis
4 *Run ___ Run*
5 *This Is the ___* with James Franco
6 "H" to Hippocrates
7 Actress Sorvino
8 Related
9 *Mike and Dave ___ Wedding Dates*
11 Eric ___ of TV's *The Last Ship*
12 Singer LaBelle
17 *Ed, ___ n Eddy*
18 Maglie and Mineo
20 *Kate ___ 8*, formerly *Jon & Kate Plus 8*
21 ___ *to Be Single* with Rebel Wilson
22 Nas's "You ___ Me" featuring Ginuwine
23 *While ___ Young* stars Ben Stiller

24 Motel of yore
25 ___*: The Lost Empire*
26 Actress Whitman of *Parenthood*
27 *Crisis in ___ Scenes* (Amazon series directed by Woody Allen)
29 Blood vessel
32 "Itsy Bitsy ___ Weeny Yellow Polka Dot Bikini"
33 "Who ___ You" by the Who
35 Shrek, for example
36 ___-Yi Previn (Mrs. Woody Allen)
37 Actor Omar ___
38 *Bates Motel* star Farmiga
39 Verdi opera
40 Fey or Turner
41 23 Across won 23 Grand ___ finals
43 Unit of conductance
44 Heidi Klum's "a"

Answers on page 118

CROSSWORD

17 ACROSS

Spell Caster

ACROSS

1 ___ of Thrones
5 Lowe or Reiner
8 "Killing Me Softly with ___ Song"
11 Coup d'___
12 Boy band ___ Direction
13 The ___ Knight Rises
14 Biblical movie featuring 17 Across
15 Pop singer who wears really long bangs
16 Cast ___ (Tom Hanks movie)
17 Hermione in the *Harry Potter* films (2 wds.)
20 "Neither a borrower ___ a lender be"
21 Half a *Law & Order* episode
24 Small workshop tool
27 Rapper ___ Rock
29 *The Real Housewives of Atlanta* star Moore
31 Said twice, a Jim Carrey movie
33 Takes too much, for short
35 "Take a ___ at Me Now"
36 Walk proudly
38 ___ Paulo, Brazil
40 CSI evidence
41 The ___ Hilton (Vietnam POW movie)
43 Actor Cage, to his friends
45 *The Perks of Being a ___* (movie starring 17 Across)
50 Miller who costarred with 17 Across in 45 Across
53 Actress Melissa ___
54 "Well, ___-da!"
55 *Finding ___* (2016 animated hit)
56 Cheers, for one
57 Luke Wilson's brother
58 ___ *Titanic* (made-for-TV movie)
59 *This Is the ___* (movie featuring 17 Across as herself)
60 "You ___?" (Lurch's question)

DOWN

1 Hackman or Wilder
2 Cartoon character ___ Ant
3 "Just the facts, ___"
4 Hawke who costarred with 17 Across in *Regression*
5 Daredevil actress Dawson
6 "Step ___!" ("Hurry up!"; 2 wds.)
7 *Beauty and the ___* (movie starring 17 Across)
8 *Hee* ___
9 *Rosemary's Baby* author Levin
10 "Lucy in the ___ with Diamonds"
13 17 Across's *Harry Potter* castmate Radcliffe
18 Pan used on *Iron Chef*
19 Mork's planet
22 "And giving ___, up the chimney he rose" (2 wds.)
23 *Lolita* star Sue ___
24 Gore and Pacino
25 *My Week ___ Marilyn* (movie featuring 17 Across)
26 Logan of *60 Minutes*
28 Letters after a dentist's name
30 Letters before an alias
32 *Project ___*
34 ___ *and Son*
37 *A View ___ Kill* (2 wds.)
39 *Lorenzo's ___* (Susan Sarandon movie)
42 "___ There" (Jackson 5 hit; 2 wds.)
44 *The ___ Purple*
46 ___ *on Me* (Morgan Freeman movie)
47 Baba ___ (Gilda Radner character)
48 *The Middle* actress Sher
49 *The Bling ___* (movie starring 17 Across)
50 Begley and Sheeran
51 Dr. Seuss's *If I Ran the ___*
52 B&O and Amtrak (abbr.)

Answers on page **118**

15 ACROSS

Fresh Prince

Answers on page 118

18 ACROSS

Comedy It Girl

ACROSS

1 Cuts the grass
5 Navy bigwig (abbr.)
8 Rapper Flavor ___
12 Actress Lena ___
13 Li'l Abner's girlfriend Daisy ___
14 *Touched by an Angel* actress Downey
15 *America's Next Top Model* 2015 winner DiMarco
16 Web address (abbr.)
17 Once more, country-style
18 *Saturday Night Live* star (2 wds.)
21 Ringo's drummer son
22 Cul-de-___
23 Ruth ___ Ginsburg (Supreme Court justice portrayed by 18 Across on *SNL*)
26 Donny and Marie
30 Life story, for short
31 Bygone airline

32 Campaign pro
33 Hillary ___ (politician portrayed by 18 Across on *SNL*)
36 *Office Christmas* ___ (2016 holiday movie featuring 18 Across)
38 Actor McKellen
39 President pro ___ of the Senate
40 Pop star portrayed by 18 Across on *SNL* (2 wds.)
46 Holliday and Severinsen
47 Sticky stuff
48 Former late-night host Jay ___
49 *Nocturnal Animals* actress Fisher
50 QVC competitor
51 Author Murdoch played by Judi Dench
52 Pal of Kenny and Kyle on *South Park*
53 Golfer's gadget
54 18 Across's *SNL* castmate Bryant

DOWN

1 Tony Shalhoub title role on TV
2 ___ Povlatsky (fictional Russian portrayed by 18 Across on *SNL*)
3 Basketball Hall-of-Famer Chamberlain
4 Go "achoo!"
5 Run ___ (go berserk)
6 "___ Horse"
7 18 Across's *Ghostbusters* castmate McCarthy
8 *Why Him?* actor James ___
9 Apple's apple, e.g.
10 Dictator Idi ___
11 Greta ___ Susteren (TV commentator portrayed by 18 Across on *SNL*)
19 Month after February (abbr.)
20 Southeast Asia war zone, to vets
23 ___ America (*Doctor Who* network)
24 Feel sick
25 "How ___ Live" (LeAnn Rimes

hit; 2 wds.)
26 *A League of Their* ___
27 *All Things Considered* radio network
28 "Itsy Bitsy Teenie Weenie Yellow Polka ___ Bikini"
29 Stallone's nickname
31 *Last Week* ___ *with John Oliver*
34 Sentra automaker
35 Body art, for short
36 Architect I.M. ___
37 Earhart or Bedelia
39 Musician-songwriter Burnett
40 18 Across's *SNL* castmate Colin ___
41 Kareem's college (abbr.)
42 Prominent Pinocchio feature
43 When repeated, a vitamin-B deficiency
44 Old-time actress Markey
45 Pink, as cheeks
46 Talk trash about

Answers on page **118**

The *SNL* star frequently played Hillary Clinton (here, in a debate sketch) and Justice Ruth Bader Ginsburg. She's also been announced to play Carole Baskin of *Tiger King* fame in a new NBC series.

20 ACROSS

Hilarious Hero

ACROSS

1 "Only Time" Irish singer
5 Damon of *Good Will Hunting*
9 ___ *Abiding Citizen*
12 *Westworld*'s Jasmyn and *Insecure*'s Issa
13 Cupid
14 Pub brew
15 Noel Coward song "Alice ___ It Again"(2 wds.)
16 Reply to the Little Red Hen (2 wds.)
17 Liam Neeson's ___-*Stop*
18 First name of 20 Across
20 *Passengers* star (with 18 Across)
22 "Made You Look" rapper
24 Dylan's "___ Went Out One Morning"(2 wds.)
25 One billion years, to geologists
28 Taylor Swift hit
30 ___ Minnelli

34 *Game of Thrones* character Jon ___
36 *Guardians of the Galaxy* with ___ Diesel (voice) and 20 Across
37 ___ Musk (electric-car pioneer)
38 Jon ___ of *Chicago P.D.*
39 Vocalist Linda ___
41 "___ It Go" from *Frozen*
42 *Blue Bloods'* Cariou
44 "Elastic Heart" singer
46 *Jurassic* ___ stars 20 Across
49 ___ *and Recreation* featured 20 Across
53 "Honest ___" Lincoln
54 Actress Laura ___
58 *The* ___ *O'Neals*
59 *Adam's* ___
60 Tennis great Nastase
61 David Bowie's "Hang ___ Yourself" (2 wds.)
62 *Manchester by the* ___
63 Plus-size model
64 *Empty* ___ (sitcom)

DOWN

1 Actor McCormack
2 Witty poet Ogden ___
3 *The Five-___ Engagement* with 20 Across
4 Sean ___ of the *Lord of the Rings* films
5 20 Across's *Delivery* ___
6 I love, in Latin
7 Prince George, e.g.
8 Frequent *Wheel of Fortune* prizes
9 ___ Del Rey
10 ___ *Like Love* (2 wds.)
11 "Zing! ___ the Strings of My Heart"
19 Claflin or Rockwell
21 Stir up
23 *The Magnificent* ___ with 20 Across
24 Hathaway and Heche
25 Double curve
26 *Rogue* ___: *A Star Wars Story*
27 Blynken's sailing pal

29 Assist
31 Mariah Carey's "___ Be There"
32 ___ Saldana (20 Across's *Guardians of the Galaxy* costar)
33 *The* ___ *Bully*
35 *The Wolf of* ___ *Street*
40 Van Winkle of folklore
43 Izzard or Redmayne
45 Actor ___ Paul
46 *Bride* ___ features 20 Across
47 Off-Broadway award
48 Actress and singer McEntire
50 ___ Russo
51 *The Vampire Diaries'* Graham and *2 Broke Girls'* Dennings
52 Piggy-bank aperture
55 Street in *Nightmare* films
56 Charlie Hunnam of *Pacific* ___
57 Nina Simone, ___ Eunice Kathleen Waymon

Answers on page **118**

14 ACROSS

Breakout Agent

Answers on page 119

ACROSS

1 Daniel ___ Kim
4 Dull-colored
8 *Quantico* organization (abbr.)
11 Slithery fish
12 Top-rated crime series *The* ___
13 Young chap
14 With 18 Across, *Quantico* star
16 *She* ___ *a Yellow Ribbon*
17 Actress Parker ___
18 See 14 Across
20 *The Last Ship* network
22 *On* ___ *Majesty's Secret Service*
23 "___ I Have This Dance?" (*High School Musical 3* song)
26 Long, long time
28 14 Across's *Quantico* castmate Aunjanue ___
32 ___ *White and the Huntsman*
34 *Les Misérables*, a.k.a. *Les* ___
36 Symbol of peace
37 14 Across's birthplace
39 *Dude, Where's My* ___?
41 Superman nemesis Luthor
42 ___ *and a Half Men*
44 Chicago ballplayer
46 U.N. program that 14 Across has participated in since 2006
49 "I ___ vacation!" (2 wds.)
53 "___ of Us" (B.o.B. song)
54 2017 beachside movie featuring 14 Across
57 Where London is (abbr.)
58 *On the Waterfront* director Kazan
59 Tamera Mowry's sister
60 *Winnie the Pooh* character
61 Say "I didn't do it!"
62 Sue Grafton's ___ *for Alibi* (2 wds.)

DOWN

1 Actor Johnny
2 With "smith," Steven Tyler's band
3 Actor Wallach and others
4 ___ Johnson (14 Across's castmate in 54 Across)
5 ___ Tin Tin
6 *Raiders of the Lost* ___
7 ___ *Blanket Bingo*
8 HGTV's *Flip or* ___
9 Actress Roseanne
10 Light bulb, in cartoons
15 "You Ain't Seen Nothing ___"
16 Miss ___ (title won by 14 Across in 2000)
19 ___ *Haw*
21 Cruise or Hanks
23 CBS forensic series
24 *Dancing with the Stars* judge Carrie ___ Inaba
25 "Wynken, Blynken and ___"
27 Actor Cage, to his friends
29 Online laugh, for short
30 "___ Been Working on the Railroad"
31 ___ *and the City*
33 Fairy-tale caster of spells
35 ___ Efron (14 Across's castmate in 54 Across)
38 *Shock and* ___
40 *Project* ___
43 Out ___ (up in the morning; 2 wds.)
45 Arthur of *The Golden Girls*
46 App-driven car service
47 Taboo
48 "Let ___" (*Frozen* song; 2 wds.)
50 Singer ___ James
51 602, in Roman numerals
52 Shouts of discovery
55 Pub drink
56 ___ and yang

15 ACROSS

Spy by Accident

ACROSS

1 *Inside the* ___
   (sports-news show)
4 Pole on a sailboat
8 *The Addams Family* cousin
11 "Woe is me!"
13 "My Way" songwriter Paul
14 *Homeland* network, for short
15 *The Spy Who Dumped Me*
   star (2wds).
17 McEwan or McKellen
18 Pasadena's Rose ___
19 *Gunsmoke's* Miss ___
21 Had dinner
22 The ___ Commandments
23 See 5 Down
26 15 Across's hubby Ashton
30 *The Book of* ___ (Denzel
   Washington thriller featuring
   15 Across)
31 *Mr.* ___ *It* (David Boreanaz
   movie)
32 *America's Next
   Top Model* host Rita

33 Hammerstein's songwriting
   partner
36 *Oz the* ___ *and Powerful*
   (fantasy movie starring
   15 Across)
38 *Much* ___ *About Nothing*
39 *Peggy* ___ *Got Married*
40 "When ___ See You Again"
   (1974 hit song; 2 wds.)
43 "___ Abe"
   (Lincoln's nickname)
46 Actress Lupino
47 Natalie Portman
   ballet movie featuring
   15 Across (2 wds.)
50 Mark Wahlberg comedy
   featuring
   15 Across
51 Woodland songbird
52 "___ on Down the Road"
   (song from *The Wiz*)
53 Horse feed
54 *House* actor Omar
55 Character voiced by
   15 Across on *Family Guy*

DOWN

1 *Apocalypse Now* setting, for
   short
2 ___ *or Flop* (HGTV makeover
   show)
3 ___ *Land* (2016 musical movie)
4 Bea Arthur role
5 With 23 Across, *Aftermath* star
6 Hit the slopes
7 "A tisket, a ___…"
8 *Michael Jackson's
   This* ___ (documentary; 2 wds.)
9 ___ *'70s Show* (sitcom starring
   15 Across)
10 ___ *n' Tina's Wedding* (movie
   starring 15 Across)
12 *Forgetting* ___ *Marshall* (movie
   featuring 15 Across)
16 Moss or Hudson
20 *Monsters,* ___
22 Menswear for the Oscars
23 *Hannah and* ___ *Sisters*
24 "Evil Woman" band,
   for short

25 *El* ___ (Charlton
   Heston epic)
26 ___ *for Killer* (ltr. & wd.)
27 Garden tool
28 Historic time period
29 The ___ Pack
31 To and ___
34 *Wonder Woman* star Gadot
35 Fit to eat
36 Gooey stuff
37 Actress Witherspoon
39 Dr. Seuss's *Fox in* ___
40 *Friends* ___ *Benefits*
   (rom-com starring
   15 Across)
41 Lightbulb, in cartoons
42 ___ Gaga
43 Angel's instrument
44 Did the Australian crawl
45 Stun with a gun
48 Once around the track
49 Positive's opposite (abbr.)

Answers on page 119

18 ACROSS

Hollywood Royalty

ACROSS

1 Kendrick Lamar's forte
4 *Charlotte's* ___
7 Israeli leader Abba ___
11 Pie ___ mode (2 wds.)
12 ___ about (approximately; 2 wds.)
14 *Bates Motel* star Farmiga
15 *This Is Where I Leave* ___
16 Actress Suvari
17 18 Across won an Oscar for ___ *Brockovitch*
18 *Money Monster* star (2 wds.)
21 Trio after L
22 Stephen Foster song "Nelly ___"
23 *Mona* ___ *Smile* stars 18 Across
26 Idris Elba's *Pacific* ___
27 Political commentator Buchanan
30 18 Across stars in ___ *Pray Love*
31 Johnny Depp's role in *The Lone Ranger*
33 Peyton Manning's brother
34 Willie Nelson's "___ Old Arms Won't Do"
35 Sue Grafton book ___ *for Outlaw* (ltr. and wd.)
36 *Notting* ___ stars Hugh Grant and 18 Across
37 Popeye's love Olive ___
38 "___ of Spades" by Motörhead
40 *The Nice Guys* star (2 wds.)
46 Actress Sorvino
47 *Heaven Is for* ___
48 Actor Kilmer
49 ___ in a poke (2 wds.)
50 Will Ferrell comedy ___-*Pro*
51 Green or Longoria
52 *The Curious* ___ *of Benjamin Button*
53 Boston Red ___
54 Stimpy's sidekick

DOWN

1 "I Hit It First" rapper (wd. and ltr.)
2 Baseball's Matty or Felipe ___
3 *Eye in the Sky* with Aaron ___
4 *Pretty* ___ (18 Across's breakout film)
5 January, to Sofia Vergara
6 U2 vocalist who's a humanitarian
7 "___ Time I Close My Eyes" by Babyface
8 Ernie's *Sesame Street* pal
9 Actresses Graynor and Meyers
10 Flossie Bobbsey's sister
13 *Who Framed Roger* ___
19 Philanthropist Hogg
20 Fuzzy red Muppet
23 Michele or Thompson
24 *The Vampire Diaries'* Somerhalder
25 Pig's digs
26 Nurses' degrees

27 Architect I.M. ___
28 Robert Redford's ___ *Is Lost*
29 "It Ain't Over '___' It's Over"
31 Woody and Mr. Potato Head, e.g.
32 Tennessee Titans (formerly Houston ___)
36 Joaquin Phoenix sci-fi rom-com
37 *August:* ___ *County* with Meryl Streep and 18 Across
38 *The* ___ (Dennis Quaid-Billy Bob Thornton drama)
39 259, to Cicero
40 a.m. TV's Kelly ___
41 *The Haj* by Leon ___
42 Spike and Ang
43 "___ the Rainbow"
44 *The 5th* ___ with Chloë Grace Moretz
45 Flair; dash
46 *Portlandia* actor Kyle ___ Lachlan

Answers on page 119

15 ACROSS

Funny Guy

ACROSS

1 *The Love* ___ (classic TV series)
5 *Before the Devil Knows You're* ___
9 One of the Kardashians
12 15 Across's *50/50* costar Kendrick
13 Stevie Wonder classic "For ___ in My Life"
14 Suffix with glob
15 Star of *Neighbors* (2 wds.)
17 Gary Oldman's ___ *by Mouth*
18 ___ *Brand Is Crisis*
19 Actor Nicolas and composer John
21 15 Across's *Pineapple Express* costar Franco
24 D, E, ___, J, K
26 "Gold" *en Español*
27 Larry David's film comedy ___ *Grapes*
29 Actress Byrne (*Neighbors* costar of 15 Across)

33 Elvis Presley's "___ Hand in Mine"
34 Ted Turner was ___ of the Atlanta Braves
36 Actress Ryan
37 *American Dream Builders* host Berkus
39 "Only Time" Irish singer
40 *Life of Pi* director Lee
41 Motivational speaker and life coach Robbins
43 *Bad* ___ with Jason Bateman
45 Sam Houston or Stephen F. Austin, e.g.
48 Will Ferrell comedy
49 Idris Elba's *Pacific* ___
50 *Magic in the Moonlight* star (2 wds.)
56 Anger
57 Objectives
58 *The Middle*'s star Sher
59 Toni Morrison is the ___ name of Chloe Wofford
60 ___ duck (outgoing official)
61 ___ *for Speed*

DOWN

1 "Last Winter" rapper
2 *Sharknado 2: The Second* ___
3 *The* ___ *Bully*
4 Lake ___, between California and Nevada
5 Jeff Bridges dramedy *The* ___ *in the Floor*
6 Chang's conjoined twin
7 ___ *Ventura: When Nature Calls*
8 Actress Judi ___
9 15 Across voices Mantis in ___ *Fu Panda*
10 Tennis great Nastase
11 Tormé and Brooks
16 Actress Rene ___
20 *Con* ___ with John Cusack
21 Lithgow or Stamos
22 Lucy Hale's *Pretty Little Liars* character ___ Montgomery
23 *A* ___ *Wanted Man*
24 ___ *People* stars Adam Sandler and 15 Across
25 *Fifty Shades of* ___

28 Luke Wilson's brother
30 *Resurrection* star Epps
31 "___ in the Clowns"
32 ___ on (goads)
35 "You'll Never Find Another Love Like Mine" singer Lou ___
38 "H" to Hippocrates
42 Hoopster Shaq's last name ___
44 Ella Fitzgerald's "Once Too ___"
45 *The Guilt* ___ (starring Barbra Streisand and 15 Across)
46 Ireland's old name
47 ___: *Days of Future Past*
48 "___ on Down the Road" from musical *The Wiz*
51 Wasikowska or Farrow
52 Cicero's 3,000
53 Horatian poem
54 Kiki Dee, ___ Pauline Matthews
55 15 Across cowrote and codirected *This Is the* ___

Answers on page **119**

18 ACROSS

Stylish Singer

ACROSS

1 Trump impersonator Baldwin
5 Baby's bed
9 *Leaving ___ Vegas*
12 Kotb of *Today*
13 Speed skater Apolo who competed on *Dancing with the Stars*
14 Envelope weight units (abbr.)
15 ___ *Crazy* (Richard Pryor film)
16 No, to Heidi Klum or Steffi Graf
17 Diesel of action flicks
18 Singer-actor with the No. 1 album *Stars Dance* (2 wds.)
21 Material that's mined
22 Sugar suffix
23 Larter or McGraw
26 Radio host Glass or lyricist Gershwin
28 Opera set in Egypt
32 TV network with a mouse-ears logo for 18 Across (2 wds.)
36 Lovato who appeared on *Barney & Friends* with 18 Across
37 Always, in poems
38 U-turn from SSW
39 Seth MacFarlane's talking-bear character
42 JFK: "___ bin ein Berliner"
44 2015 financial-crisis film featuring 18 Across in a cameo (3 wds.)
49 *Horton Hears a ___!* (18 Across's voice-role movie)
50 Test
51 *Gone with the Wind* plantation
53 "Good for ___" (18 Across song)
54 Kelly who's bantered with Regis and Michael
55 Supply-and-demand subject (abbr.)
56 Hockey great Bobby
57 ___ *Choice Awards* (honors won multiple times by 18 Across)
58 Dunham of *Girls*

DOWN

1 Sounds that doctors make you say
2 Plenty
3 Falco of *The Sopranos*
4 *Monte ___* (18 Across movie named for a Riviera resort)
5 Sean who played James Bond
6 Perlman of *Cheers*
7 *The Princess Bride*: "My name is ___ Montoya. You killed my father. Prepare to die"
8 Chaz and Sonny
9 "Same Old ___" (18 Across hit)
10 Ansari of *Parks and Recreation*
11 Nine-digit ID issued at birth (abbr.)
19 Buffalo's lake
20 ___ *Girls* (Lindsay Lohan film)
23 Use a calculator
24 Tell fibs
25 Commercial suffix
27 ___ *Ventura: Pet Detective*
29 *Holiday ___*
30 Lion's lair
31 Friar Tuck drink
33 Nick at ___
34 Famed annual college-football award
35 St. Louis landmark structure
40 Siskel's "two thumbs up" partner
41 *The ___ Chicks*
43 ___ *Transylvania* (with 18 Across voicing Dracula's daughter)
44 Superhero title role for Chris Hemsworth
45 Jackie Chan in *Rush ___*
46 Slack-jawed stare
47 *The Amazing ___*
48 Combo CGI/live-action sci-fi film
49 Cheyenne's state (abbr.)
52 Ortiz of *Ugly Betty*

Answers on page 119

20 ACROSS

Scandal Fixer

ACROSS

1 Grand ___ (home run with bases loaded)
5 The ___ We Were
8 Oodles (2 wds.)
12 Online-video site
13 Mineral
14 Infomercial how-to
15 ___ After (Drew Barrymore movie)
16 Mr. & ___ Smith (movie featuring 20 Across)
17 ___ Girls (Lindsay Lohan movie)
18 Harper Valley ___
20 With 21 Across, Scandal star
21 See 20 Across
26 The ___ ("Love Train" singers)
27 Sons of Anarchy actor Perlman
28 "That hurts!"
31 Herbert of The Pink Panther
32 Jamie Foxx biopic featuring 20 Across
33 Grand ___ Opry
34 Memo abbreviation
35 Place for ChapStick
36 J. ___ (Leonardo DiCaprio biopic)
38 I Think I ___ (Chris Rock movie costarring 20 Across; 3 wds.)
40 The X-___
43 V for Vendetta actor Stephen
44 Don't Look Now director Nicolas
45 Carrey or Parsons
47 The 40-___-Old Virgin
51 Miracle at St. ___ (movie featuring 20 Across)
52 Brian of Roxy Music
53 20 Across's For Colored Girls castmate Anika ___ Rose
54 Best Actress Oscar winner Patricia
55 Emeril catchword
56 All's Well That ___ Well

DOWN

1 ___ Hate Me (Spike Lee movie starring 20 Across)
2 2012 movie starring Common
3 Pub drink
4 Eddie of A Thousand Words, costarring 20 Across
5 Superheroine Wonder ___
6 Airport abbr.
7 Ouija-board option
8 Don Draper, Roger Sterling, etc.
9 Creepy look
10 Sharif or Epps
11 20 Across's Scandal castmate Goldwyn
19 "___ the season to be jolly"
20 ___-Tiki
21 The ___ of Wall Street
22 "A thing of beauty is ___ forever" (2 wds.)
23 Blue Bloods actress ___ Gayle
24 What's Eating Gilbert ___
25 ___ Story 3
28 Mr. Bear of Jellystone Park
29 Frozen snowman
30 ___ the Millers (Aniston-Sudeikis comedy)
32 6 Rms ___ Vu (Carol Burnett TV movie)
35 NCIS: ___ Angeles
36 ___ of the Beholder (Ashley Judd movie)
37 ___ Johnson, aka the Rock
38 Boston ___ (series that featured 20 Across)
39 Michael Keaton comedy (2 wds.)
40 The Nanny star Drescher
41 Actress Skye
42 Game of Thrones star ___ Headey
45 George W.'s brother
46 TV chef ___ Garten
48 Long, long time
49 Harry Potter ___ the Goblet of Fire
50 Sue Grafton's ___ for Ricochet (ltr. and word)

Answers on page 119

16 ACROSS

Beloved Actor

ACROSS

1 16 Across voiced
a vehicle named Woody in it
5 Many a character in *Aladdin* or
Ben-Hur
9 Grier of *Jackie Brown*
12 Help, in a crime
13 The Beatles' lovely meter maid
14 Darth Vader's childhood
nickname
15 Movie clownfish that Marlin
wants to find
16 He made a big splash in
Big and *Splash* (2 wds.)
18 "Help me, ___-Wan Kenobi"
20 Jumps for Gracie Gold
21 16 Across movie with
a color and a distance
in its title (3 wds.)
26 ___ and Juliet
27 Farrow and Hamm
28 Ouija-board word that's English
for *oui* and *ja*
29 Arthur of *Golden Girls*

30 Longoria of *Telenovela*
33 New York sports-radio
station (the last
three letters are a synonym
for enthusiast)
35 Sean who played
the hobbit Sam
37 16 Across movie named for a
Pennsylvania city
40 "___, come back!" (classic
western line)
41 College transcript number
(abbr.)
42 16 Across voiced Sheriff
Woody in it (2 wds.)
45 ___ *Away* (16 Across deserted-
island movie)
49 *Ready Player* ___:
50 Movie scene shown
on a talk show
51 Great Lake that Ohio abuts
52 Horror-film director Craven
53 Miami's NBA team
54 The Village People's
four-letter song

DOWN

1 *Catch Me If You* ___
(16 Across movie)
2 Grampa Simpson
3 "Losing My Religion" band
4 Moe, Larry or Curly
5 *Glee*'s Abrams or bandleader
Shaw
6 2016 Olympics site
7 Bank dispenser (abbr.)
8 "Kokomo" lyric "Bermuda, ___,
come on pretty mama"
9 Celebrity group on *Match
Game*, e.g.
10 Shackled body joint
in *Cool Hand Luke*
11 *Little* ___ *Sunshine*
17 ___ & Allies (WWII game)
19 Mario to Luigi, briefly
21 Shakira's *Zootopia* song "___
Everything"
22 Dirt-turning tool
23 Ambulance letters (abbr.)
24 Change, as a script

25 Vardalos or Peeples
29 Black sheep's nursery-rhyme cry
30 Biblical verb ending
31 *Final Fantasy* ___ (sixth sequel)
32 Tennis's Ivanovic
33 Comes out on top
34 L.A. reporter title role for
Chevy Chase
35 *The Sound of Music* mountain
36 *Se7en* psychopath villain
Kevin ___
37 "E.T. ___ home"
38 Acting great Helen
or President Rutherford
39 Cleopatra country
40 Put cargo on board
43 Bullfight cheer
44 Coastal inlet
46 The murderer in
The Fugitive had only one
47 Reporter's (typo not fixed) word
48 Leoni of *Madame Secretary*

Answers on page 119

18 ACROSS

Storm Star

¹	²	³		⁴	⁵	⁶		⁷	⁸	⁹	¹⁰	¹¹
¹²				¹³				¹⁴				
¹⁵				¹⁶				¹⁷				
¹⁸			¹⁹			²⁰						
	²¹					²²			²³	²⁴	²⁵
²⁶	²⁷			²⁸	²⁹			³⁰			
³¹			³²				³³		³⁴		
³⁵		³⁶		³⁷				³⁸			
³⁹			⁴⁰				⁴¹				
		⁴²		⁴³	⁴⁴				⁴⁵	⁴⁶	
⁴⁷	⁴⁸	⁴⁹		⁵⁰				⁵¹			
⁵²				⁵³				⁵⁴			
⁵⁵				⁵⁶				⁵⁷			

ACROSS

1 *Ferris Bueller's Day* ___
4 Old Navy's owner
7 Singer Sledge or Faith
12 Sacha Baron Cohen's *Da* ___ *G Show*
13 "Eureka!"
14 ___ cologne (2 wds.)
15 Peg for Tiger Woods
16 *Sports Illustrated* output, for short
17 Ed who voiced the old man in *Up*
18 Oscar winner for *Monster's Ball* (2 wds.)
21 Tiny bit of moisturizing cream
22 *Balto* or *Into the Wild* setting
26 Superhero role for 18 Across
30 Fly high
31 Tax return month (abbr.)
32 *The Whole Nine* ___
34 Prefix with "verse"

35 Injure severely
37 Director of 18 Across's first film, *Jungle Fever* (2 wds.)
39 Texas border city in *No Country for Old Men* (2 wds.)
41 Social or capital suffix
42 She played Rogue alongside 18 Across's Storm (2 wds.)
47 ___ Anton Ohno
50 Title for Ridley Scott or Ben Kingsley
51 Disco ___ of *The Simpsons*
52 Moody Blues hit with the lyric "We've already said goodbye" (2 wds.)
53 DIY's *The Vanilla* ___ *Project*
54 "Ew, gross!"
55 Strong glue
56 Diana Prince, ___ Wonder Woman (abbr.)
57 Beret-wearing activist Guevara

for pageant host Steve Harvey

DOWN

1 Inauguration Day recitation
2 Toto or Benji biter, perhaps
3 School expedition in an early *Spider-Man* scene (2 wds.)
4 Handheld Nintendo device popular in the '90s (2 wds.)
5 *Moby Dick* captain
6 Ellen of *Juno*
7 *Girl with a* ___ *Earring*
8 ___ pie (really simple; 2 wds.)
9 Compete in a 10K
10 Do-re-mi notes
11 "___ darn tootin'!"
19 ___ *& Order*
20 "Amazing" magician
23 Genre sometimes linked with R&B (2 wds.)
24 Danity ___ (MTV's *Making the Band* group)
25 Singer India. ___
26 Romantic comedy *Along* ___ *Polly* (2004)

27 "C'mon, be ___" ("Help me out"; 2 wds.)
28 Kourtney's oldest son (or lawyer Perry ___)
29 Dada artist Jean
33 Locale with slopes and lifts (2 wds.)
36 "___ moment" (antacid catchphrase)
38 Title after an attorney's name (abbr.)
40 *The Man from* ___ *River*
43 *Kung Fu Panda* and *Godzilla* continent
44 Justin Bieber's "___ Me"
45 *The Seven Year* ___
46 *War Games* missile, for short
47 The number in PG-13 or NC-17
48 Dr. Seuss's *Hop on* ___
49 Singer Yoko

Answers on page **119**

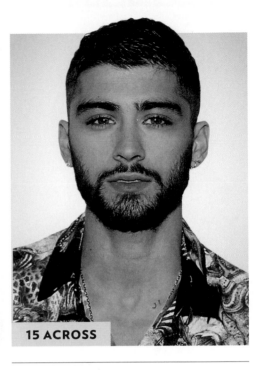

15 ACROSS

British Singer

ACROSS

1 Toto's wagger
5 ___ Like It Hot
9 Pampering locale the *Real Housewives* might visit
12 Antimugging spray
13 "___ the night before Christmas . . ."
14 Ziering of *Sharknado*
15 Former One Direction singer whose name is an anagram for "a lazy mink" (2 wds.)
17 Make faces for the camera
18 Habit wearer in *The Sound of Music*
19 Aussie actress Kidman
21 Sci-fi film: ___ *the Worlds* (2 wds.)
24 Stately Wayne ___ (Batman's mansion)
25 Talent show where 15 Across got his break (3 wds.)
29 Not happy
30 ___ *& Order: Special Victims Unit*
31 ___ Tai (tropical drink)
34 15 Across's No. 1 solo debut (a.k.a. bedroom chatter)
38 ___ *Dad* (military-themed sitcom)
41 Golfer Palmer, familiarly
42 Magazine staffer who revises articles
44 Hamm or Farrow
45 Scottish cap
46 One Direction No. 1 hit: "What Makes You ___"
51 "Er-r . . ."
52 2 to 1, at the Kentucky Derby
53 Cyrano de Bergerac had a large one
54 "Gangnam Style" singer
55 Meat Loaf's "You ___ the Words Right Out of My Mouth"
56 "Coming ___ to a theater near you"

DOWN

1 Celebrity gossip site
2 Skinny battery size
3 Like a frozen roadway
4 Eurythmics singer Annie
5 Laurel of Laurel and Hardy
6 Hooter in *Harry Potter* films
7 ___ Street, U.S.A.
8 Igloo dweller
9 Cowell who signed One Direction
10 São ___, Brazil
11 ___ *Management*
16 Hand or ear warmer
20 *Gran Torino* vehicle
21 Lbs. and oz. (abbr.)
22 Type of "moment" Oprah might have
23 ___ *Riding Hood*
26 One Direction's *Up ___ Night*
27 Baseball great Ripken Jr.
28 *A Tale of ___ Cities*
31 Film-title word after *Iron*,

Ant or *Spider*
32 Boxer Muhammad
33 Eisenhower's nickname
34 Pile of chips in *The Sting* or *Rounders*
35 Will Smith movie based on an Isaac Asimov book (2 wds.)
36 Thriller classic ___ *Until Dark*
37 *Planes,* ___ *and Automobiles*
38 Had a rendezvous (2 wds.)
39 Amy of *Big Eyes*
40 Fallon who booked 15 Across for his debut solo appearance
43 Change, as the decor
44 Tesla CEO Elon
47 Hubbub
48 ___ Fighters (rock band)
49 Troops-entertaining group (abbr.)
50 Carrie Ann and Bruno's judging pal

Answers on page **119**

17 ACROSS

Funny and Fearless

ACROSS

1 Beer barrel
4 *20,000 Leagues Under the* ___
7 17 Across's *Inside Out* castmate Hader
11 Movie theater concession choice
12 *The 40-Year-___ Virgin* (movie featuring 17 Across)
13 The Beatles' "___ in the Life" (2 wds.)
14 *Rectify* star ___ Young
15 *The Bourne Identity* organization (abbr.)
16 *Terminator 3:* ___ *of the Machines*
17 Actress-comedian who voiced Disgust in *Inside Out* (2 wds.)
20 "___ a Rebel" (1962 hit song)
21 Critical hospital area (abbr.)
22 17 Across's *The Mindy Project* costar Messina

25 "___ Night" (Maroon 5 song; 2 wds.)
29 Tic-tac-toe crossing
30 Jane Lynch's *Glee* character
31 HGTV *Design Star* judge Vern ___
32 17 Across's *Inside Out* castmate Amy
35 *Wreck-It ___* (animated movie featuring 17 Across's voice)
37 *Up in the* ___
38 "Hold on a ___!"
39 He played 17 Across's boss on *The Office* (2 wds.)
44 Give off, as light
46 "A long time ___ in a galaxy far..."
47 Ronnie Howard role
48 Lymph ___
49 ___ King Cole
50 Farm structure
51 *The ___ Hunter*
52 *Rizzoli & Isles* network
53 ___-fi

DOWN

1 *The Road* actor ___ Smit-McPhee
2 *East of* ___
3 1982 Oscar-winning movie
4 Dr. Seuss's *Fox in* ___
5 *On the Waterfront* director Kazan
6 *The Age of* ___ (Blake Lively movie)
7 Showman P.T. ___
8 "___ Rock and Roll Music" (2 wds.)
9 *Fear and Loathing in* ___ *Vegas*
10 Strong soap ingredient
11 Rockwell or Elliott
18 *Say ___ to the Dress*
19 Rapper-actor ___-T
22 *Kindergarten* ___ (Schwarzenegger comedy)
23 "Yoo-___!"
24 ___ *vs. Wade* (Holly Hunter TV movie)
25 *Days of* ___ *Lives*

26 Popeye's girlfriend Olive ___
27 Actor Torn
28 Corey Stoll's *The Strain* role
30 Mr. Carson or Mrs. Patmore in *Downton Abbey*, e.g.
33 "Mad" *Alice in Wonderland* character
34 Tell a whopper
35 *V for Vendetta* star Stephen
36 ___ *the Universe* (2007 Beatles-based movie)
38 Michael ___ (39 Across's *The Office* role)
39 *The Blind* ___ (Sandra Bullock movie)
40 Actor Christopher of *Dominion*
41 Movie on a grand scale
42 Leslie Caron 1953 title role
43 DiCaprio's nickname
44 *This Is the* ___ (movie featuring 17 Across)
45 One of the Three Stooges

Answers on page **119**

After creating and acting in six seasons of *The Mindy Project*, the star (seen here with Chris Messina, who played her beau) became mom to a daughter, Katherine, and in 2020 a son, Spencer.

30 ACROSS

Man of Action

ACROSS

1 The Cardinals, on scoreboards
4 Item an actor holds
8 Record label for, appropriately, Rogers, Cyrus and Aguilera
11 Garr or Hatcher
12 Word in a Mozart title that precedes (and rhymes with) "kleine"
13 Long time period
14 "Rub-a-dub-dub, three men in ___" (2 wds.)
15 30 Across in The ___ King (named for a venom-tailed creature)
17 30 Across's wrestling ring name (2 wds.)
19 *Spamalot* author Eric ___
20 Agent Gold in *Entourage*
21 "No ___" (Chinese menu phrase)
23 Ray's wife in *Everybody Loves Raymond*
26 ___ *Hollywood* (Michael J. Fox film)

27 Guffaw syllable
30 Former wrestler who voiced Maui in *Moana* (2 wds.)
33 "Ready, ___, go!"
34 Coveted fuel in *The Road Warrior*
35 Sty sounds
36 Type of doctor in *The Incredible Dr. Pol,* for short
37 *The Simpsons* bartender
38 Prefix with perspirant
41 30 Across's NFL-themed HBO series
45 30 Across in *Race to Witch* ___
48 Travel à la Columbus or Captain Jack Sparrow
49 ___ *Can Cook* (Chinese cooking show)
50 Children's classic *The ___ in the Willows*
51 Cable sports award
52 Drama series *Murder ___ Wrote*
53 *Eyes Wide Shut* party
54 *Bill ___ the Science Guy*

DOWN

1 MacFarlane or Meyers
2 ___ *Grit*
3 The New York Public ___ (book-filled shelter in *The Day After Tomorrow*)
4 Joe of *Goodfellas*
5 Politician Perry or Santorum
6 Singer Yoko
7 Pay-___-view
8 *Sharknado* actress Tara ___
9 LL ___ J
10 *Green Gables* girl
11 Body art, slangily
16 Porky or Petunia
18 ___ *Is the New Black*
21 Sound from Elsie or Elmer
22 TV movie *High ___ Musical*
23 Dental degree (inits.)
24 Female sheep
25 Word before mobile or man, in Gotham City
26 Radio personalities, briefly

27 QVC competitor
28 Astronaut's thumbs-up
29 ER assistants (abbr.)
31 Try a dish, on Bravo's *Top Chef*
32 Big name in television ratings
36 Diesel of *xXx*
37 Patinkin of *Homeland*
38 Schumer and Poehler
39 Biblical ark builder
40 *Name That ___* (game show)
41 Crosby of *Holiday Inn*
42 ___ *Rider* ('60s Peter Fonda movie)
43 Ready for picking, as fruit
44 Stallone's nickname
46 Boys Like Girls (feat. Taylor Swift) hit "___ Is Better Than One"
47 On ___ (TV studio sign)

Answers on page **119**

16 ACROSS

Singing Idol

ACROSS

1 Like the head of Mr. Clean or Elmer Fudd
5 ___ *Smart*
8 Teeth on a gear
12 HBO's ___ *Blood*
13 *Tangled* song "___ Got a Dream"
14 Video game (or ring-shaped structure in it)
15 State school near Beverly Hills (abbr.)
16 With 18 Across, *Dreamgirls* star
18 See 16 Across
20 Map close-up
21 Fine Young Cannibals' "___ Drives Me Crazy"
22 CSI sample (abbr.)
23 Overly competitive (wd. & letter)
26 Honey holder for Pooh
27 Surface for skater Gracie Gold
30 Movie in which 16/18 Across played Carrie Bradshaw's assistant (4 wds.)
33 Dads
34 Nickname of theatre cat in *Cats* (his full name is a spear-shaped veggie)
35 Beastie Boys' "Make Some ___"
36 *Doctor* ___ (sci-fi series)
37 Suffix with Silver for a line of Chevy pickups
38 "I'm cuckoo for ___ Puffs!"
41 *NBC Nightly News* anchor before Brian Williams
44 With 46 Across, TV competition that launched 16/18 Across's career
46 See 44 Across
48 Lancelot and Galahad
49 *Suits* network
50 Sneaker with a swoosh logo
51 ASAP on *E.R.*
52 Candy in a cartoon-character dispenser
53 Beano alternative (hyph.)

DOWN

1 A/C unit (abbr.)
2 Half of the golden pair at McDonald's
3 Woman's name that also means humdinger
4 The ___ Scrolls (ancient Middle East writings; 2 wds.)
5 Military action figure (inits. & name)
6 ___ *Stevens*
7 Melissa d'Arabian's ___ *Dollar Dinners*
8 *The* ___ *Syndrome*
9 Klutzes
10 Fox musical series set in a high school
11 U2's "A ___ of Homecoming"
17 Mario and Luigi's company
19 City preceding *Noon* and *Knights* in two Jackie Chan titles
22 Homer's "oops"
23 Recipe amount (abbr.)
24 Vote in favor of
25 Military stores, briefly
26 Scoreboard numbers (abbr.)
27 Episode number of the sixth *Star Wars* movie
28 Dollar parts (abbr.)
29 "___ of the Tiger"
31 Laverne and Shirley or Ren and Stimpy
32 ___ Channel (Food Network alternative)
36 *What's the* ___ *That Could Happen?*
37 Lucy's partner Desi
38 Mama ___ Elliot
39 Leave out
40 Michael of *Superbad*
41 1st, 2nd or 3rd, on a diamond
42 Sara McLachlan hit
43 Stir-fry pans
45 Kevin Costner in *Tin* ___
47 Superman nemesis ___ Luthor

Answers on page 119

15 ACROSS

Dreamgirls Guy

<table>
<tr><td>1</td><td>2</td><td>3</td><td>4</td><td>■</td><td>5</td><td>6</td><td>7</td><td>8</td><td>■</td><td>9</td><td>10</td><td>11</td></tr>
<tr><td>12</td><td></td><td></td><td></td><td>■</td><td>13</td><td></td><td></td><td></td><td>■</td><td>14</td><td></td><td></td></tr>
<tr><td>15</td><td></td><td></td><td></td><td>16</td><td></td><td></td><td></td><td></td><td>■</td><td>17</td><td></td><td></td></tr>
<tr><td>■</td><td>■</td><td>■</td><td>18</td><td></td><td></td><td></td><td>■</td><td>■</td><td>19</td><td>20</td><td></td><td></td></tr>
<tr><td>21</td><td>22</td><td>23</td><td></td><td></td><td>■</td><td>24</td><td>25</td><td></td><td></td><td></td><td>■</td><td>■</td></tr>
<tr><td>26</td><td></td><td></td><td></td><td>■</td><td>27</td><td>28</td><td></td><td>■</td><td>■</td><td>29</td><td>30</td><td>31</td><td>32</td></tr>
<tr><td>33</td><td></td><td></td><td></td><td>■</td><td>34</td><td></td><td></td><td>■</td><td>35</td><td>■</td><td>36</td><td></td><td></td></tr>
<tr><td>37</td><td></td><td></td><td>38</td><td>■</td><td>39</td><td></td><td></td><td></td><td></td><td>■</td><td>40</td><td></td><td></td></tr>
<tr><td>■</td><td>■</td><td>41</td><td>42</td><td></td><td></td><td></td><td>■</td><td>43</td><td>44</td><td></td><td></td></tr>
<tr><td>45</td><td>46</td><td>47</td><td></td><td></td><td></td><td>48</td><td></td><td></td><td>■</td></tr>
<tr><td>49</td><td></td><td></td><td>■</td><td>50</td><td>51</td><td>52</td><td></td><td></td><td>■</td><td>53</td><td>54</td><td>55</td></tr>
<tr><td>56</td><td></td><td></td><td>■</td><td>57</td><td></td><td></td><td></td><td>■</td><td>58</td><td></td><td></td></tr>
<tr><td>59</td><td></td><td></td><td>■</td><td>60</td><td></td><td></td><td>■</td><td>61</td><td></td><td></td></tr>
</table>

ACROSS

1 David ___ Pierce
5 Exam
9 ___ Abiding Citizen stars 15 Across
12 Human-rights lawyer Clooney
13 Sunburn remedy
14 "Put ___ Happy Face" (2 wds.)
15 Star of Sleepless (2 wds.)
17 15 Across's Oscar film
18 ___-Man with Paul Rudd
19 "___ to Build a Dream On" classic song (2 wds.)
21 Kirsten ___ of Hidden Figures
24 Arnaz or Arnaz Jr.
26 "___ Buttermilk Sky"
27 Biographer Leon ___
29 The Walking ___
33 Actor Bentley
34 Will Smith's I, ___
36 Boxer's biopic with 15 Across
37 Basketball's Brooklyn ___
39 Game-cube creator Rubik
40 Narrow river inlet
41 Rae of Insecure
43 Django Unchained stars 15 Across and Christoph ___
45 Actress Linney
48 Bon Jovi's "___ of Roses"
49 ___-Margret
50 Collateral costar of 15 Across (2 wds.)
56 Queen Latifah's ___ It Off
57 "Not ___ Thing" by Justin Timberlake (2 wds.)
58 ___ Who's Talking
59 "Just the ___ of Us"
60 ___ Lives with Kevin Spacey
61 "Elmer's ___"

DOWN

1 The ___ by Leon Uris
2 Soprano with great range ___ Sumac
3 Grand Coulee or Hoover
4 Inventor ___ Howe
5 27th U.S. President
6 "Livin' Thing" band
7 Chicago White ___
8 ___ Killing Fields with Jessica Chastain
9 Shark Tank's Greiner
10 Ortiz and Gasteyer
11 A Million ___ to Die in the West
16 Bruce Lee classic ___ the Dragon
20 Ben Stiller's The Heartbreak ___
21 White House ___ stars 15 Across
22 Peter Fonda's ___'s Gold
23 One Flew over the Cuckoo's ___
24 Messing or Winger
25 Musk of electric-car fame
28 Celine Dion's "Where ___ My Heart Beat Now"
30 James ___ Jones
31 Dismounted
32 Cameron ___ (2014 Annie costar of 15 Across)
35 ___ Heist with Eddie Murphy
38 Sean Connery's title
42 Beelzebub
44 Young ___ with Charlize Theron
45 Vin Diesel's The ___ Witch Hunter
46 "The Promise of ___ Day" by Paula Abdul (2 wds.)
47 Golden Rule preposition
48 A-F connection
51 A sash for a Japanese kimono
52 The Amazing Spider-___ 2 with 15 Across
53 Jimmy Dean or Lee Greenwood tune
54 Channing Tatum's The ___ of No One
55 ___ out a living

Answers on page 119

9 ACROSS

Former Housewife

ACROSS

1 *Over Her ___ Body* (9/16 Across movie)
5 Madonna's "___ Don't Preach"
9 With 16 Across, Miss Corpus Christi of 1998
12 Ashton's wife before Mila
13 Car service that's booked via smartphone
14 ___-com (film genre, for short)
15 Tiger Woods's ex Nordegren
16 See 9 Across
18 TV athletic awards
20 Nonfiction films, slangily
21 Football or hockey
24 "___ looking at you, kid"
25 *Desperate ___* (9/16 Across series)
29 "The Best Is ___ to Come"
30 Sunshade for Phil Mickelson or Maria Sharapova
31 2005's *Monster-in-___*
34 9/16 Across NBC sitcom about a Spanish soap opera
36 Computer accessory (hyph.)
39 Clint Eastwood in *The ___ Sanction*
40 Like unsweetened cranberries
41 "Am not!" comeback (2 wds.)
44 ___ *Nine Nine* (sitcom 9/16 Across guest-starred on)
46 Singing great Minnelli
50 Off-road four-wheeler, for short
51 Online auction site
52 Barbara of *I Dream of Jeannie*
53 Word before both "Young" and "Restless" in a 9/16 Across soap
54 Singer Del Rey
55 The NBA's Parker, once married to 9/16 Across

DOWN

1 President monogram between HST and JFK
2 Shrieking fish in *The Princess Bride*
3 Taylor Swift's "___ Ready for Love" (2 wds.)
4 Guy Fieri's ___, *Drive-Ins and Dives*
5 ___ *Fiction*
6 Johnny Cash's "___ Named Sue" (2 wds.)
7 Bank items attached to chains
8 *Evita* country (abbr.)
9 Mistake
10 *The ___* (show hosted by Carson Daly)
11 Stockpile
17 Poems of praise
19 Spielberg or Seagal
21 Like Adrian in *Rocky*, painfully at first
22 Author Edgar Allan
23 Pixar's *Inside ___*
24 Sci-fi series "reborn" as a miniseries in 2015
26 Syfy's *The ___ Wheaton Project*
27 Suffix with "expert"
28 Diane ___ Furstenberg
31 KFC piece
32 Quaff in *Robin Hood*
33 *World ___ Z*
34 Kansas dog that traveled by tornado
35 The "v" of Roy G. Biv
36 Appearance at home plate (2 wds.)
37 Title for Vader or Maul
38 "The Night They ___ Old Dixie Down"
41 Jessica of *Honey*
42 Macklemore's partner Lewis
43 Award-winning Irish singer for "May It Be"
45 *Kenan & ___* (late-'90s Nickelodeon sitcom)
47 Vow words (2 wds.)
48 "___ Ball Master" (*Kung Fu Panda 2* song)
49 ___ *Which Way You Can* (1980 film starring Clint Eastwood)

Answers on page 119

CROSSWORD

19/20 ACROSS

Mysterio Man

ACROSS

1 Mountains in *The Grand Budapest Hotel*
5 Thurman of *Pulp Fiction*
8 Campus outcast who got revenge in a 1984 movie title
12 Toucan Sam's "nose"
13 Actor-director ___ Howard
14 ___ 51 (military facility in *Independence Day*)
15 Ivy League university in New York City that 19/20 Across attended
17 Lena Dunham's ___ *Furniture*
18 Mauna___ (Hawaiian volcano)
19 With 20 Across, star of *Everest*
20 See 19 Across
25 McClanahan of *Golden Girls*
26 *The ___ Queen* (1952)
30 Like most car radios (letters)
32 ___ *Pepper's Lonely Hearts Club Band*
33 Cannes coin
34 Boris's partner in *The Adventures of Rocky and Bullwinkle*
36 Parsons of *The Big Bang Theory*
37 2011 sci-fi movie with 19/20 Across (2 wds.)
41 With 45 Across, dude-ranch comedy in which 19/20 Across played Billy Crystal's son
43 From ___ Z (2 wds.)
44 *The Amazing ___*
45 See 41 Across
50 "Somewhere ___ the Rainbow"
51 Barbie's sometime beau
52 Dave Matthews Band: "The ___ of You"
53 Kentucky Derby wagers
54 "___-haw!" (western cry)
55 *Monday Night Football* broadcaster

DOWN

1 *The View* network
2 DiCaprio, to friends
3 Buddy
4 ___ Island (*King Kong* setting)
5 Country star Keith
6 Miss Piggy's "Me?"
7 Ortiz of *Ugly Betty*
8 Portman of *Black Swan*
9 Estrada who played Ponch
10 Actress Russo
11 *The ___ After Tomorrow* (19/20 Across movie)
16 Larry and Curly's fellow Stooge
19 Skippy or Jif holder
20 ___ *Torino*
21 *3:10 to ___*
22 Imagine Dragons' "Nothing ___ to Say"
23 "Horrible" comic-strip character
24 Toward the rear, in *Titanic*
27 Stephen King title about a rabid dog
28 Dry, like the Sahara
29 Alaska town where the Iditarod dogsled race ends
31 Showtime's ___ *of Sex*
32 Moo ___ pork
35 Type of sauce at a sushi bar
38 Michael who played Alfred in *The Dark Knight*
39 And so on (abbr.)
40 TV political newswoman Roberts
41 Batman's hangout, for example
42 Coco's costar in an E! reality show (hyph.)
44 Brat Pack's Lowe
45 *October ___* (19/20 Across movie)
46 Ang who directed 19/20 Across in *Brokeback Mountain*
47 Asner and Harris
48 Street cred
49 *Grand Theft Auto: ___ Andreas*

Answers on page **120**

18 ACROSS

Colombian Comic Star

ACROSS

1 *Modern Family* network
4 Speak like Don Corleone
8 Manhattan-based fashion label (ltrs.)
12 Michele of *Glee*
13 *Survivor* or *Cast Away* setting
14 Start of a phrase for Popeye (2 wds.)
15 The "p" of mph
16 Sean who played Ned Stark in *Game of Thrones*
17 Stonestreet of *Modern Family*
18 She played Gloria on *Modern Family* (2 wds.)
21 *Leaving ___ Vegas*
22 Brit's bathroom, slangily
23 Spanish-language network for 18 Across
27 Trail behind
30 Cyndi Lauper 1983 hit "Girls Just Want to Have ___"
31 *Paul Blart: Mall ___* (2009)
32 Bigheadedness

33 *Air Force ___*
34 HBO vampire series for Joe Manganiello (2 wds.)
37 Arthur of *Golden Girls*
38 Ziering of the *Sharknado* movies
39 English soccer star in a Diet Pepsi ad with 18 Across (2 wds.)
45 Dr. in the *Austin Powers* movies
46 Alison of *Mad Men* (or a type of cheese)
47 R&B singer ___ Charles
49 Nick once married to 18 Across
50 Doubled, a Jim Carrey film
51 Dr. of rap
52 Not ___ many words (2 wds.)
53 Deputy in *The Dukes of Hazzard*
54 Gives a thumbs-up, briefly

DOWN

1 Swiss peak
2 *The Secret Life of ___*
3 Kennedy who was ambassador to Japan
4 Giovanni of *Avatar*
5 On the ocean
6 Czech or Pole
7 Cruz of *Vicky Cristina Barcelona*
8 San ___, Calif. (just north of Tijuana)
9 Sedgwick of *The Closer*
10 Brand of hair-removing cream
11 Four-letter Village People hit
19 Best-liked, in online shorthand
20 Burgundy in *Anchorman*
23 Sci-fi ship (inits.)
24 What Whoopi dressed as in *Sister Act*
25 "Triple word score" game
26 Poker game chit

27 DiCaprio of *Django Unchained*
28 "Four score and seven years ___ . . ."
29 England's "___ Save the Queen"
34 Seth MacFarlane's talking bear
35 *Sons of Anarchy* Harley riders, for example
36 "Well, ___-di-dah"
37 Baggins in *The Hobbit*
39 Pastrami-on-rye seller
40 Mary Kay rival
41 Competes
42 *Dancing with the Stars* host Andrews
43 "Goodbye," in Italian films
44 Wahlberg of *Wahlburgers*
48 "Owner of a Lonely Heart" band

Answers on page **120**

15 ACROSS

Funny Father

ACROSS

1 Supply company in *Road Runner* cartoons
5 *Quantum* ___ (sci-fi series)
9 Chemical tub, such as in *Suicide Squad*
12 ___ *Husbands of Hollywood* (15 Across show)
13 Sheriff Taylor's boy
14 Clint Eastwood's *Letters from ___ Jima*
15 Star of *Paper Soldiers* (2 wds.)
17 Dr. Seuss's *If I ___ the Zoo*
18 Vardalos of *My Big Fat Greek Wedding*
19 ___ *Movie 3* (horror comedy for 15 Across)
21 Boy
24 *Mad Money* network
27 ___ mobile (opposite of "news")
28 Movie set in Brazil: *Blame It ___* (2 wds.)
30 *The ___ of Living Dangerously*
32 *Meet the Parents* sequel that featured 15 Across (2 wds.)
37 Ward of *Sisters*
38 Cicely or boxer Mike
39 Decorative pillow cover
42 Kendall and Kylie Jenner's mom
44 Elected official, briefly
45 Madea actor ___ Perry
47 Poe's *The Murders in the ___ Morgue*
49 ___ Speedwagon
50 Rapper who costarred with 15 Across in *Soul Plane* (2 wds.)
56 Newswoman Curry
57 Jugular or varicose follower
58 Actress Falco or McClurg
59 ___ *the Dog*
60 *Star Wars* escape vehicles
61 *One Flew over the Cuckoo's ___*

DOWN

1 Boat in 2014's *Noah*
2 ___ Lo Green
3 Dallas hoopster, briefly
4 Tiger Woods's ex-wife
5 Lindsay of *Mean Girls*
6 Org. that monitors oil spills (abbr.)
7 ___ *Force One*
8 *The Secret Life of ___* (film 15 Across voiced)
9 Like videos that spread rapidly
10 BET ___ (prize on a show 15 Across hosted in 2011)
11 Broadway statuettes
16 Kidman of *The Hours*
20 ___ Sherwood (Faith Ford's *Murphy Brown* role)
21 Texter's guffaw
22 Singer DiFranco
23 ___ *& the Women* (2 wds.)
25 Overwhelmingly (2 wds.)
26 Company head (abbr.)
29 "Who's there?" reply (2 wds.)
31 Misbehaves (2 wds.)
33 Thranduil's antlered mount in *The Hobbit*
34 Sixth sense (inits.)
35 Pooh and Piglet's pal
36 "Live from New York…" show (inits.)
39 The Scarecrow's stuffing in *Oz*
40 One of a villainous trio in *The Lion King*
41 Word before "Came Polly" or after "Ride" in 15 Across movie titles
43 Jeremy of *Batman v Superman: Dawn of Justice*
46 Invitation reply letters
48 *East of ___*
51 *The Matrix* hero
52 Planet suffix
53 "___ to Billy Joe"
54 Soldiers in *Patton,* for short
55 ___ *Smart*

Answers on page **120**

1 ACROSS

One of a Kind

ACROSS

1 Only person to win a Grammy, Emmy and Best Actress Oscar
5 Abbr. preceding Fuji and Everest
8 "___ to the Chief"
12 Kathie Lee's morning cohost
13 "___ moment" (Oprah phrase)
14 Prefix with plasm in *Ghostbusters* and *Topper*
15 Curry and Coulter
16 1988 Ryan-Quaid remake (also an ER status abbr.)
17 Dr. of daytime TV
18 Sonny & 1 Across's signature song (4 wds.)
21 Bruno Mars's "It Will ___"
22 *Law & Order:* ___
23 *This Film Is Not ___ Rated*
25 Houston-to-Chicago compass direction
27 Adrien of cosmetics
31 Bluto in *Animal House,* for example
33 iPhone add-on
35 Number before 10
36 Estée Lauder fragrance White ___
38 Farm ___ (benefit concert since 1985)
40 *Guardians of the Galaxy* actress Saldana
41 JFK's successor (inits.)
43 1 Across's son
45 1 Across's *Moonstruck* costar (2 wds.)
49 What an ent (in *Lord of the Rings*) resembles
51 Vegas preceder
52 ___ *Season* (animated movie)
53 Schreiber of *Salt*
54 ___ and outs
55 Watermelon exterior
56 *The Da Vinci* ___
57 Self-pride
58 NBA team from Brooklyn

DOWN

1 Starbucks classic ___ tea latte
2 *The Road to ___ Kong*
3 Ralph Kramden's pal (2 wds.)
4 Many a Bob Marley fan
5 "Vogue" singer
6 *O Brother, Where Art ___?*
7 Turbo 900 cars
8 Audrey who was a role model for 1 Across
9 Feel the aftereffect of a spin class
10 "That's ___ Quit—I'm Movin' On" (2 wds.)
11 Texter's alternative to "ha ha"
19 Yang's opposite
20 Gardner once married to Sinatra
23 Designer handbag monogram
24 Giants QB Manning
26 Smog-fighting govt. org. (abbr.)
28 "When the moon hits your eye like a big ___ . . ." (2 wds.)
29 Suffix with Angel for a Hollywood resident
30 Mötley Crüe drummer Tommy
32 1 Across's only Grammy-winning song, in 2000
34 *Guernica* artist Pablo
37 Jimmy Fallon network
39 Batting-only A.L. players (abbr.)
42 Angelina of *Maleficent*
44 Nut that conks Chicken Little
45 OneRepublic's "Something I ___"
46 1992's "Constant Craving" singer k.d.
47 Lady's partner, briefly
48 Shel Silverstein's book of poems *Where the Sidewalk* ___
49 *Little People, Big World* network
50 Home of the 2016 Summer Olympics, for short

Answers on page **120**

21 ACROSS

Funny Lady

ACROSS

1 Folksinger Baez
5 *America's ___ Talent*
8 Sharpen
12 David Bowie's "Hang ___ Yourself" (2 wds.)
13 DiFranco of folk rock
14 Baseball's Rodriguez, for short
15 "___ Wild Heaven" by R.E.M.
16 Bryce Dallas Howard's dad
17 Exploit
18 Julia Roberts's ___ *Pray Love*
20 Singer Furtado
21 Comedian-actress-writer-producer (2 wds.)
26 Singer Bonnie ___
27 Hanks Williams biopic *I ___ the Light*
28 *Scandal* network
31 Rumpelstiltskin, e.g.

32 Diana King's "___ Guy"
33 Twelve dozen (abbr.)
34 Ansel Adams and Andre Agassi's monograms
35 Enemy
36 Neil Diamond's "I Am . . . ___" (2 wds.)
38 Confrontational comedian nicknamed Mr. Warmth (2 wds.)
40 ___ *Crimes*
43 *Scream Queens'* Michele
44 Elvis ___ Presley
45 Tina Turner's ex
47 *The ___ with the Lower Back Tattoo* (book by 21 Across)
51 ___ in (slow a horse)
52 Yasiin Bey, a.k.a. Mos ___
53 ___'s *Anatomy*
54 Kevin ___ (*Inside . . .* TV costar of 21 Across)
55 Animated film *The ___ Bully*
56 "No Ordinary Love" singer

DOWN

1 21 Across had a recurring role in ___ Glaser's *Delocated*
2 Anne Hathaway's ___ *Day*
3 "One Piece ___ Time" by Johnny Cash
4 ___ for the weary (2 wds.)
5 Country singer Brooks
6 The Plastic ___ Band
7 *Cat on a Hot ___ Roof*
8 *Barry's* Bill ___
9 Pitcher-turned-sportscaster Hershiser
10 Oasis rocker Gallagher
11 *Ed, Edd n ___*
19 *Sister ___*
20 *Orange Is the ___ Black*
21 Song for Andrea Bocelli
22 "___ Cass" Elliot
23 Barks shrilly
24 "Climax" R&B singer
25 *What Dreams ___ Come*
28 "I've Got ___ in Kalamazoo" (2 wds.)

29 21 Across's *Trainwreck* costar Larson
30 Food fishes
32 Scott Eastwood, to Clint
35 Rom-com *One ___ the Money*
36 ___ *Age: Collision Course*
37 Bluegrass singer-songwriter Ricky ___
38 English poet John ___
39 "___ My Heart in San Francisco" (2 wds.)
40 21 Across cohosted *A Different Spin with ___ Hoppus*
41 No Smoking ___
42 "___ Together" by the Who
45 First Lady McKinley
46 *The Night Shift's* Leung
48 Gershwin or Levin
49 ___ *Dawn* with Chris Hemsworth
50 Soap input

Answers on page **120**

14 ACROSS

Prime-Time Anchor

ACROSS

1 Major network where 14 Across got his start
4 ___ *favor* (please, in Spanish)
7 "___ Jude" (Beatles song)
10 Boring
11 Lady sheep
12 Carvey or Delany
13 Annapolis initials
14 With 16 Across, popular CNN journalist
16 See 14 Across
18 Marco Rubio's state (abbr.)
19 Gretchen of *Boardwalk Empire*
20 Actor-comedian Patton ___
24 14 Across's fellow *60 Minutes* correspondent Lara
27 ___ la la
28 Christmas tree type
29 Elvis's middle name
30 Caesar or Vicious
31 What 39 Across uses as a garage
32 Henpeck
33 Army cops
34 *Dancing with the Stars* dancer Hough
35 14 Across's mother, ___ Vanderbilt
37 Conservative talking head Coulter
38 Hockey legend Bobby
39 ___ *v Superman: Dawn of Justice* (movie in which 14 Across plays himself)
43 Game show on which 14 Across was a celebrity contestant
47 14 Across's fellow *60 Minutes* correspondent Charlie
48 Fashion designer Tahari or Saab
49 Takes too much, for short
50 "Put ___ on it!" (2 wds.)
51 ___ *There Was You* (1997 rom-com)
52 *Scream* director Craven
53 Football Hall-of-Famer Dawson

DOWN

1 *The Sun ___ Rises*
2 Bath, in Spanish
3 Piper's last name in *Orange Is the New Black*
4 ___ *Harbor* (Ben Affleck WWII movie)
5 "On My ___" (Miley Cyrus song)
6 Sundance Kid portrayer Robert
7 *Rumor ___ It…*
8 Musician Brian
9 TV show ___ *Can Cook*
10 Tampa Bay footballer, for short
12 *Win, Lose or ___*
15 *Born Free* lioness
17 Long, long time
21 Out yonder
22 ___ *with Kelly* (show that 14 Across has cohosted)
23 *Star ___*
24 Singer k.d.
25 Shakira's ___ Fixation Tour
26 Singer Belinda Carlisle was one
27 "___ the season to be jolly"
30 Johnny Depp's *Pirates of the Caribbean* role Jack ___
31 Cable's Comedy ___
33 Actress Sorvino
34 *CSI* evidence
36 Hitchcock thriller
37 *The ___* (underwater sci-fi movie)
40 *The ___* (game show hosted by 14 Across in the early 2000s)
41 Z ___ zebra (2 wds.)
42 Actor Beatty
43 Sully's Airbus, e.g.
44 Quarterback Manning
45 What they call "Texas tea"
46 Presidential initials of the 1950s

Answers on page 120

18 ACROSS

Cooking Queen

ACROSS

1 Boring
5 Punker Vicious or funnyman Caesar
8 *Bonanza* brother (or, slangily, a cowpoke's mount)
12 ___ 911!
13 *Much ___ About Nothing*
14 State where the *Field of Dreams* field was
15 Tirade
16 Stewart or Cryer
17 Sound off like MGM's mascot
18 Bravo cooking-competition host (2 wds.)
21 History Channel's *The Curse of ___ Island*
22 Ad ___ committee
23 Tom Colicchio, on 33 Across, or Howie Mandel, on *America's Got Talent*
26 Author Salman, once married to 18 Across

30 Verse prefix, in a beauty pageant title
31 "___ whiz!"
32 Toward the back in *Mutiny on the Bounty*
33 Cooking show that 18 Across hosts (2 wds.)
36 Country where 18 Across was born
38 *The Fault in ___ Stars*
39 Angsty music genre
40 Hollywood restaurateur who's guested on 33 Across (Mozart had the same first name)
46 "___ We Never Said Goodbye" (2 wds.)
47 One kicked up by a Rockette
48 Simmons of 33 Across
50 Floating ice sheet
51 Dr. of rap
52 English queen or princess
53 After ring, a smartphone sound
54 *The ___ Couple*
55 Allen (of *Chopped*) and Danson

DOWN

1 Shiverer's sound
2 Amy Adams in ___ *Year*
3 Paquin or Faris
4 Type of bun in *Sausage Party* (2 wds.)
5 Pat who says "spin or solve"
6 *American ___*
7 Phil who paved the way for Oprah
8 Actor Emile or Judd
9 Intrigued sound
10 Competed à la Michael Phelps
11 Bollywood wrap
19 Double entendre champ West
20 Decisions in *Raging Bull,* for short
23 Stick (out)
24 Start of U2's "Vertigo": "___, dos, tres…"
25 Backward-bending move on *DWTS*
26 *Rocky* ring official

27 Seth MacFarlane's *American ___!*
28 "___ were king of the forest…" (2 wds.)
29 Due-in approximation (abbr.)
31 Rivera of Fox News
34 *Comedians in Cars Getting ___*
35 Two-armed embrace
36 Little *World of Warcraft* demon
37 Chewy white candy bar ingredient
39 Attacked so that the yolk's on them
40 Drift, as an aroma
41 Norway's capital
42 Cowardly Oz character
43 Geeky revenge-getter in a movie title
44 Charlie Chaplin stick
45 *Close Encounters of the Third ___*
49 ___ *Misérables*

Answers on page **120**

In 2020 the *Top Chef* host launched a series about the many U.S. food traditions, *Taste the Nation*, and said, "I finally got to show the world what I would do if I got to build a show from scratch."

13 ACROSS

Mother Monster

ACROSS

1 Chump
4 "___ Romance" (13 Across hit)
7 In the Heart of the ___
10 Hathaway or Heche
11 "To ___ is human…"
12 "___ Dance" (13 Across hit)
13 *Superstar* singer-songwriter (2 wds.)
15 ___ upon a Time
16 Nastiness
17 Sharif or Epps
19 ___ Flew over the Cuckoo's Nest
21 "Respect" singer
25 Tony who recorded the Cheek to Cheek album with 13 Across
29 ___ Atlas (Tom Hanks movie)
30 Grand ___ Opry
31 The Last ___ bender

33 Gun enthusiasts' group (abbr.)
34 Big kiss
37 ___: A Dame to Kill For (movie featuring 13 Across; 2 wds.)
40 American ___ Story (series featuring 13 Across in season 5)
42 ___ constrictor
43 Movie like Star Wars, e.g.
45 Astronaut's path around Earth
49 "Poker ___" (13 Across hit)
52 Petula Clark hit of 1965
54 CHiPs star Estrada
55 "…___ he drove out of sight…"
56 Historic time periods
57 Marry
58 The Catcher in the ___
59 E.R. workers (abbr.)

DOWN

1 Rice Krispies sound
2 "You ___" (13 Across hit; 2 wds.)
3 Quarterback Manning
4 Who Wants to ___ Millionaire (2 wds.)
5 Oscar-winning Ben Affleck movie
6 Daytime ___ (soap opera)
7 Under the Tuscan ___ (Diane Lane rom-com)
8 Key on your computer keyboard
9 "I can't believe I ___ the whole thing!"
10 Pacino and Madrigal
12 Superman's birth father
14 Hackman or Wilder
18 Rainbow shape
20 Greek letter
22 Collette or Braxton
23 The ___ Locker (2009 Oscar winner)
24 The Beatles' "___ in the Life" (2 wds.)
25 "Nonsense!"

26 Giggly Muppet
27 Don't Go ___ the Water
28 "___ the season to be jolly"
32 Adam's ___ (Spencer Tracy-Katharine Hepburn classic)
35 Dawson's ___
36 "Keystone" lawman of silent films
38 High ___ (Gary Cooper western)
39 Helena Bonham ___
41 Pale ___ (Clint Eastwood movie)
44 Glee actor Monteith
46 ___ This Way (13 Across album and hit song)
47 ___ a Teenage Werewolf (2 wds.)
48 2,000-lb. weights (abbr.)
49 A ___ Good Men (starring Jack Nicholson)
50 "We ___ the World" (1985)
51 El ___ (Charlton Heston movie)
53 "In the ___ Small Hours of the Morning" (Frank Sinatra song)

Answers on page **120**

15 ACROSS

SNL Alum

ACROSS

1 *Gotham's* ___ Pinkett Smith
5 "___ My Train a Comin'" by Jimi Hendrix
9 Make a choice
12 Earned an A
13 Fuzzy red Muppet found on *Sesame Street*
14 ___ Tse-tung
15 Comic-actor host of the 88th Academy Awards (2 wds.)
17 Pooh's pal Eeyore, e.g.
18 Chesney or Rogers
19 *After* ___ with Will Smith
21 News journalist Curry
23 Eddie Murphy's *48* ___
24 15 Across is writer-director-star of ___ *Five*
27 Allman Brothers Band hit album ___ *Peach* (2 wds.)
29 15 Across's *I Think I Love My* ___
33 ___ *of State* with 15 Across
35 2009 rom-com *He's Just* ___ *That Into You*
36 Baseball's Slaughter
37 ___ Stanley Gardner
38 "The First ___" (carol)
40 *Beverly Hills* ___ *II* with 15 Across
41 Schumer or Poehler
43 Chris Hemsworth's *In the Heart of the* ___ (2015)
45 Actress-model Stewart
48 Dostoyevsky's *The* ___
52 "Snap Yo Fingers" rapper ___ Jon
53 *Grace and Frankie* costar of Lily Tomlin (2 wds.)
57 *Telenovela's* Longoria
58 Redding of soul music
59 *The Lion King's* sound
60 The "C" in C.I.A. (abbr.)
61 Completely engrossed
62 "Only Time" Irish singer

DOWN

1 Nicholson or Black
2 Steady pain
3 Bruce ___ of *The Hateful Eight*
4 "Freak Like Me" singer Howard
5 *In* ___ *Shoes* with Cameron Diaz
6 Band now known by its initials
7 *The Walking Dead* network
8 The *Today* show's Al ___
9 Actor Epps
10 *X-Men: Days of Future* ___
11 TV's ___ *O*
16 "Auld Lang ___"
20 The Monkees' "___ Go Along" (2 wds.)
22 ___ *McPhee* with Emma Thompson
23 15 Across co-created *Everybody* ___ *Chris*
24 Gina Rodriguez of *Jane* ___ *Virgin*
25 "___ the ramparts we watched…"
26 ___ *Joey*
28 *Think Like a Man* ___
30 *Monsters,* ___
31 ___ Fighters (band)
32 Mental telepathy, e.g.
34 *Hit the Floor* actor Cain
39 Explorer Erikson
42 ___ *Crimes* with Mary McDonnell
44 "___ You" by Miley Cyrus
45 *Concussion's* Baldwin
46 *Saturday Night* ___ starred 15 Across for three years
47 Country singer Jackson
49 Privy to (2 wds.)
50 Jazz vocalist Anita ___
51 Wallace or Reid
54 *Death* ___ *Funeral* with 15 Across (2 wds.)
55 Dylan Walsh of ___ */Tuck*
56 Time in New York's zone (inits.)

Answers on page 120

15 ACROSS

British Import

ACROSS

1 Just fine, to an astronaut
4 Captain played by Gregory Peck
8 ___ Me In (vampire movie)
11 The ___ (Get Smart bad guy)
13 A Knight's ___ (Heath Ledger movie)
14 "To ___ is human…"
15 Luther star (2 wds.)
17 "___ a yellow ribbon…"
18 Singer-actress Reese
19 ___ to the System (Michael Caine movie; 2 wds.)
21 "Oops!…I ___ It Again" (Britney Spears song)
23 Early Beatle Sutcliffe
24 Mandela: Long Walk to ___ (movie starring 15 Across)
28 "___ Lady" (Tom Jones song; 2 wds.)
32 The ___ C (Laura Linney show that featured 15 Across)

33 ___ Girl (Zooey Deschanel sitcom)
35 Porky or Babe, e.g.
36 "The fault, dear Brutus, is not ___ stars…" (2 wds.)
39 Acclaimed crime series that featured 15 Across (2 wds.)
42 Greek letter
44 Singer Yoko
45 The No. 1 ___ Detective Agency (series that featured 15 Across)
48 Stomach problem
52 Roxy Music cofounder
53 Steve Carell sitcom that featured 15 Across in 2009 (2 wds.)
56 Much ___ About Nothing
57 Don't ___ Mom the Babysitter's Dead
58 To be, in French
59 Pacific ___ (sci-fi flick starring 15 Across)
60 "___ and Sound" (Sheryl Crow song)
61 Actor Brynner

DOWN

1 ___ reflux
2 Ye ___ Tea Shoppe
3 Lagerfeld or Malden
4 Grabbed a bite
5 2001 computer
6 Actress Jessica and family
7 ___ of No Nation (movie starring 15 Across)
8 Actor Jared
9 Bana or Roberts
10 Star ___ Beyond (movie featuring 15 Across)
12 Olivia or Oscar
16 Enough ___ (Julia Louis-Dreyfus movie)
20 "Excuse me?"
22 Cheadle or Knotts
24 Designated Survivor investigating agency (abbr.)
25 ___ Tin Tin
26 Sense of self
27 How I ___ Your Mother

29 Prefix with Pen or logue
30 Michael Caine's title
31 Avengers: ___ of Ultron (movie featuring 15 Across)
34 Horton Hears a ___!
37 Mentalist ___ Geller
38 Gone with the Wind's Butler and namesakes
40 Plenty, slangily
41 Detective Nero ___
43 Ice Cube's real first name
45 Shakespeare's King ___
46 Lady Gaga's "You ___" (2 wds.)
47 Indiana Jones and the Temple of ___
49 Sex and the ___
50 Beige shade
51 The Crash ___ (snowboarding documentary)
54 Will Ferrell Christmas comedy
55 Grand ___ Opry

Answers on page 120

16 ACROSS

Designing Woman

ACROSS

1 Bruno Mars's "Just the Way You ___"
4 The genie's home in *Aladdin*
8 Kiefer, to Donald Sutherland
11 Second-place finisher to a tortoise
13 Falco of *The Sopranos*
14 Place to get a pint in *Local Hero*
15 The Grateful Dead's kind of rock
16 With 18 Across, celeb once known as Posh
18 See 16 Across
20 Wallach of *The Deep*
21 ___ *Cartoon President*
22 The ___ Connection
25 With 35 Across, pop group for Posh
28 Wins in which one boxer doesn't get up, briefly
29 Slime
30 RPM measurer on a dashboard, for short
31 ___ *and the City*
32 Sound that Catwoman might make
33 Mined material
34 "You've got mail" company (inits.)
35 See 25 Across
36 Indiana's pro-basketball team
38 Live or Farm follower for a concert
39 Ron Weasley's pet Scabbers, for one
40 16/18 Across's birth country
44 ___ *Idol* (16/18 Across was a guest judge on it in 2010)
47 Summer Olympics sword
48 Leoni of *Madam Secretary*
49 "___, señor!" (2 wds.)
50 The ___ *Housewives of Dallas*
51 Nightmare street of filmdom
52 *Little Man* ___
53 ___ Lanka

DOWN

1 *Moby-Dick* captain
2 *The Amazing* ___
3 Ivanka and Donald Trump Jr.'s brother
4 Burton of *Star Trek: TNG*
5 Take ___ view of (2 wds.)
6 Open-___ night (for stand-up wannabes)
7 Broadway star Bernadette
8 Jerry of trash TV
9 Yes, at the Cannes Film Festival
10 LeBron's league (abbr.)
12 N.Y.C. mayor whose name is an anagram of "choked" (2 wds.)
17 Cheer that David 18 Across often heard
19 Tint
22 Actor Michael J. ___
23 ___ *Hand Luke*
24 Third Eye Blind's "___ It Going to Be?"
25 ___ *Making Sense* (Talking Heads movie)
26 Legal or medic prefix
27 Scoopful in a cone (2 wds.)
28 Kenan's TV partner
31 ABBA hit that's also a *Titanic* distress call
32 Bette a.k.a. the Divine Miss M
34 Van Gogh or Monet
35 Booking for a band
37 One of two atop Bugs Bunny's head
38 "Tomorrow" musical
40 ___ *of Eden*
41 *Planet of the* ___
42 The Beach Boys' "Don't Go ___ the Water"
43 Place to order a Milton Berle (along with a kosher dill)
44 Had a meal
45 ___ C (nickname for Sporty 25 Across)
46 *Clear and Present Danger* org.

Answers on page 120

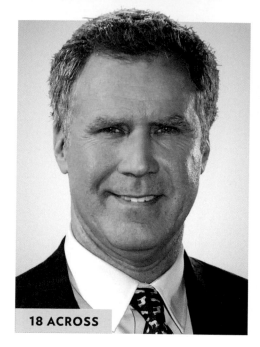

18 ACROSS

Lead Anchor

ACROSS

1 *The ___ in the High Castle*
4 *The Other ___* stars 18 Across
8 British singer Woolley
12 "Don't Bring Me Down" band (abbr.)
13 Louisa May Alcott poem "Here's ___" (2 wds.)
14 *Did You ___ About the Morgans?*
15 Actor Cheadle
16 ___ Kedrova of *Zorba the Greek*
17 Architect Saarinen
18 Comic-actor in 140 *SNL* episodes, 1995-2015 (2 wds.)
21 Myrna ___ of the *Thin Man* films
22 ___ *Andreas* with Dwayne Johnson
23 Paul ___ (*Anchorman 2: The Legend Continues* costar of 18 Across)
26 *Eye in the ___*
27 Presidential aspirant Bush
30 Mahershala ___ of *Moonlight*
31 *The Diary of Samuel ___*
33 Pindar poem, e.g.
34 ___ *Max: Fury Road*
35 *Arrival* star Adams
36 Kings of ___ (band)
37 Street in a horror-film series
38 Scooby-___
40 *The Tonight Show Starring ___* (2 wds.)
45 18 Across's *Daddy's ___*
46 *La La ___*
47 Scott Joplin creation
49 Aerosmith's "Love ___ Elevator" (2 wds.)
50 "Just ___" by Quincy Jones
51 "The dog ___ my homework"
52 *A Beautiful ___* with Russell Crowe
53 Exploiter
54 Idina Menzel's "___ It Go"

DOWN

1 *Chicago ___* with Oliver Platt
2 Keenan Ivory Wayans's ___ *Down Dirty Shame* (2 wds.)
3 Anika ___ Rose
4 Actor-director Vincent ___
5 Consolidate; fuse
6 *Elf* is a ___tide comedy with 18 Across
7 ___ *& Hutch*
8 Michael or Charlie
9 Shoe part
10 *Me and ___ and the Dying Girl*
11 Semi-___ stars 18 Across
19 Honorary law degree
20 Romano and Liotta
23 L.A. team member
24 Ending for spat
25 *Why ___ I Get Married Too?*
26 Melissa McCarthy comedy
27 Actor Manganiello
28 Tokyo's former name
29 ___ Stiller's *Zoolander 2* features 18 Across
31 Grease one's ___ (bribe)
32 Country singer Harris
36 "Laughing out loud" in chatroom shorthand
37 Alter; correct
38 TV's ___ *Moms*
39 Jeff Bridges's ___ brother Beau
40 Singer-songwriter Mitchell
41 Somali supermodel and cosmetic pioneer
42 Red carpet event observers
43 ___ Roberts University
44 Interior designer Berkus
45 *Why ___?* with James Franco
48 ___ *Hard* stars Kevin Hart and 18 Across

Answers on page **120**

18 ACROSS

Trump Portrayer

ACROSS

1 30 ___ (18 Across sitcom)
5 Modern music genre in *Hamilton*
8 Spill the beans
12 Slangy suffix with switch
13 Hot flake spewed out in *Volcano*
14 Cowboys QB Tony
15 Harry Potter's lightning-shaped mark, for example
16 1002, in Roman numerals
17 Double Stuf cookie
18 Emmy winner for 1 Across (2wds.)
21 Shakespeare's *Much ___ About Nothing*
22 Ray-___ sunglasses
23 Aslan, Simba and Mufasa
26 ___: *Impossible—Rogue Nation* (18 Across film)
30 Treelike *Lord of the Rings* creature
31 Bronzed from the sun
32 Daft Punk or Indigo Girls
33 *The Hunt for Red ___* (18 Across film)
36 ___ *Landing* ('80s TV show for 18 Across)
38 Actor Stephen ___, whose last name is an anagram of 53 Across
39 "Aw ___, it was nothing"
40 Scottish actor who played a Russian sub captain in 33 Across (2 wds.)
45 Amish structure raised in *Witness*
46 *Girls* network
47 One Direction's "___ He Know?"
49 As limp as ___ (2 wds.)
50 Horror film street
51 *Damn Yankees* temptress
52 ___ *of the Guardians* (18 Across film: voice)
53 Carly ___ Jepsen
54 Cable sports network

DOWN

1 Hi-___ scan
2 Killer whale or the shark-hunting boat in *Jaws*
3 ___ *Miner's Daughter*
4 The ___ War (*M*A*S*H* setting)
5 Stallone's Vietnam-vet role
6 Bollywood continent
7 Regis who worked alongside Ripa
8 California governor Jerry and TV's Campbell ___
9 Loughlin or Petty
10 Prayer-ending word
11 Radley in *To Kill a Mockingbird*
19 Songs are burned on them
20 ___ *Boot* (German film with a 98 percent Rotten Tomatoes rating)
23 DiCaprio, familiarly
24 Zach Braff's *Alex, ___*
25 Baseball great Mel
26 Trump's ___-a-Lago
27 Words 18 Across and Kim Basinger once exchanged (2 wds.)
28 Pixar's *Inside ___*
29 Thumbs-down responses
31 *Bad ___*
34 ___ *Is the New Black*
35 Stiller of *Zoolander*
36 Barbie's beau
37 Item with an eye on *Project Runway*
39 Travelocity's red-coned figure
40 Garment often worn by women in South Asia
41 Notable time periods
42 Syllables before "di" and "da" in a Beatles song (hyph.)
43 Hopping Aussie animals, informally
44 Crowd-sourced review website
45 Supermodel Refaeli
48 ___ Diego Comic-Con

Answers on page **121**

18 ACROSS

'Delicate' Songstress

ACROSS

1 Grampa Simpson
4 Francis of Assisi and Teresa of Avila, e.g. (abbr.)
7 Facebook button
11 *Lara Croft:* ___ *Raider*
13 Longtime CBS forensic series
14 Jai ___
15 ___ mater
16 "Everything ___ Changed" (18 Across hit)
17 *Dead* ___ (Nicole Kidman thriller)
18 Grammy-winning singer-songwriter (2 wds.)
21 Tic-tac-toe crossing
22 ___ and yang
23 "I Knew You Were ___" (18 Across hit)
27 Took a selfie
31 *The Bachelorette* network

32 Health resort
34 *Selma* director DuVernay
35 Guantanamo, for short
38 "___ Don't Care" (song featuring 18 Across and Keith Urban)
41 *Inside* ___ (Pixar animated film that won 2016 Oscar for Animated Feature)
43 *Norma* ___
44 One Direction singer who dated 18 Across (2 wds.)
49 Pie à la ___
50 52, Roman-style
51 "We Are Never ___ Getting Back Together" (18 Across hit)
53 "___ Eyes" (18 Across hit)
54 *A Nightmare on* ___ *Street*
55 ___ *to Five* (Lily Tomlin comedy)
56 *Girls* creator Dunham
57 ___ v. *Wade*
58 British "Inc."

DOWN

1 *One Day* ___ *Time* (2 wds.)
2 Animated pooch voiced by John Travolta
3 *Harry Potter* actress Watson
4 Alice Cooper's "___ Out"
5 Russian ruler, in the old days
6 Spacek of Netflix's *Bloodline*
7 *The Godfather* actor Al
8 *Frozen* snowman
9 2010 Angelina Jolie movie
10 "___ McGraw" (18 Across's debut single)
12 Linda Ronstadt's "Blue ___"
19 High shot in tennis
20 Reddi-___ (dessert topping)
23 Kids' running game
24 Baseball stat (abbr.)
25 Month after September (abbr.)

26 Corey Stoll's *The Strain* role
28 *The Last Time I* ___ *Paris*
29 Actress Longoria
30 *Valentine's* ___ (movie featuring 18 Across)
33 TV show's spot
36 *Gotham* actress Baccarin
37 "___ Song" (18 Across hit)
39 Marcia ___ Harden
40 Actress Mirren
42 Madea's creator ___ Perry
44 ___ *Floats* (Sandra Bullock movie)
45 *Rectify* star ___ Young
46 Farm structure
47 *Midnight in the Garden of Good and* ___
48 E-mailed
49 Gretchen of *Boardwalk Empire*
52 "Colorful" 18 Across album

Answers on page **121**

The singer-songwriter (at the 2019 AMA Awards) surprised fans with her eighth album, *Folklore*, during the 2020 shutdown. "In isolation my imagination has run wild, and this album is the result," she said.

CROSSWORD

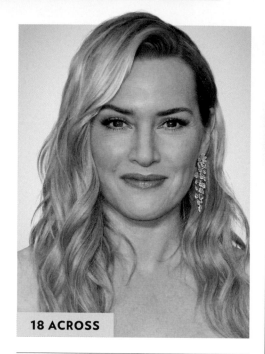

18 ACROSS

Titanic Talent

¹	²	³	■	⁴	⁵	⁶	■	⁷	⁸	⁹	¹⁰

(crossword grid — numbered squares 1–52)

ACROSS

1 "For Me and My ___"
4 Depot, for short
7 Sinatra's "___ Old Saturday Night"
11 ___ of the World (Jane Hamilton bestseller; 2 wds.)
13 "Mark Twain" is a ___ de plume
14 Country music's Jackson
15 U2's frontman
16 Strangers ___ Train (2 wds.)
17 The Outsider's Jared
18 Collateral Beauty and Steve Jobs star (2 wds.)
21 Gore and Green
22 The ___ After Tomorrow
23 LaBelle and Austin
26 18 Across's The Holiday costar Jude
27 Oft-quoted Chairman
30 ___ James (Insurgent and Divergent costar of 18 Across)
31 Two, to Salma Hayek
32 18 Across's Finding Neverland costar Johnny
33 "Like a ___ Song" by John Denver
34 Nickname for 18 Across's Titanic costar
35 Wilder and Hackman
36 Golden Girls actress Arthur
37 Obsolete, for short
38 The Americans star (2 wds.)
43 "Heart Attack" singer Lovato
44 Escape-key letters
45 Revolutionary ___ stars 18 Across
47 Plus-size model
48 Little, to Scottish poet Robert Burns
49 Hatcher, Polo or Garr
50 Orbison and Clark
51 Basketball's N.C. ___ Heels
52 Dustin Hoffman film ___ the Dog

DOWN

1 Chew the fat
2 Run ___ (go wildly awry)
3 Singer Del Rey
4 The ___ of Kilimanjaro
5 Singer Braxton
6 Peet and Plummer
7 Astronaut Ride
8 Skipper's direction at sea
9 18 Across's Contagion costar Damon
10 Rock composer Brian
12 Mr. ___ Head (Toy Story character)
19 Peyton Manning's brother
20 Horror film with six sequels
23 Post-traumatic stress (inits.)
24 "Eureka!"
25 MacFarlane bear movie
26 "Too-Ra-___-Ra-Loo-Ral (That's an Irish Lullaby)"
27 Children of ___ with Clive Owen
28 Tarzan's pal Cheeta, e.g.
29 Photo ___ (picture-taking sessions)
31 Mommie ___
32 Sahara or Gobi
34 Don Ho's neck wreath
35 Dramatist Shaw's monogram
36 Actress Larson and wrestler Bella
37 Award won by 18 Across for The Reader
38 Tonto calls the Lone Ranger ___ sabe
39 Award won by 18 Across for Mildred Pierce
40 West Point letters
41 Movie-theater mogul Marcus
42 Good Morning America's Spencer
43 James Van ___ Beek
46 Archaeological ___ (probing excavation)

Answers on page 121

22 ACROSS

Texan Star

ACROSS

1 Movie
5 Civil rights leader with a January holiday (inits.)
8 Musical about an auntie
12 ___ 51 (UFO movie)
13 The CBS logo represents one
14 Border on
15 "You ___?" (Lurch's line in *The Addams Family*)
16 Michele of *Glee*
17 Danson and Koppel
18 Cookbook author Garten
20 Food for Scrat the squirrel in *Ice Age*
22 Oscar-winning *Dallas Buyers Club* star (first name at 8 Down)
27 ___ pal (female bestie)
28 *To ___, with Love*
29 Macho guy
31 Not much, as of paint (2 wds.)
33 Snakelike fish in *The Princess Bride*
35 Game-show line: "You've just ___ new car!" (2 wds.)
36 ___ Jessica Parker
38 Short snooze
40 Explosive-sounding cable channel
41 *My Cousin Vinny* Oscar winner who played 22 Across's ex in *The Lincoln Lawyer* (2 wds.)
44 Incidentally, in a text
45 Marriage vow (2 wds.)
46 *Aida* solo
49 Dog sound, notably from Orphan Annie's
51 *Fool's ___* (22 Across movie)
55 Hitchcock's ___ *Window*
56 Sheep sound
57 Peter Fonda's honey-collecting role
58 Stone of *The Help*
59 Librarians' shushing sound
60 Kings of ___ (band)

DOWN

1 Take 5's "Never ___ Away"
2 George Gershwin's songwriting brother
3 *Dancing with the Stars* judge Goodman
4 ___ *Mike* (22 Across movie)
5 Actress Griffith
6 Soap-making ingredient
7 Reeves of *The Matrix*
8 22 Across's first name
9 Honest Prez, for short
10 "Dirty" coming-of-age movie for 22 Across
11 Sci-fi aliens, briefly
19 Negative responses
21 "Yuck!"
22 Téa Leoni in ___ *Secretary*
23 Santa ___ University (soccer-scholarship school in *Bend It Like Beckham*)
24 Madison Square Garden, for one
25 Overact
26 *Live at the Acropolis* new-age musician
27 Car-tank filler
30 Turner in 2016's *The Birth of a Nation*
32 Walters who interviewed 22 Across in her 2006 special
34 "Queen" who interviewed 22 Across on her talk show
37 Blockbuster
39 ___ people (*Invasion of the Body Snatchers*)
42 Cleans the *Black Pearl*'s deck
43 Movie bigwig
46 *We ___ Marshall* (22 Across movie)
47 Michael Stipe's band
48 Will Smith in ___ *Legend* (2 wds.)
50 Cheerleader's cheer
52 Bullfight chant
53 DiCaprio, to friends
54 Lion's hangout

Answers on page 121

17 ACROSS

Forever 'Flawless'

ACROSS

1 Billy ___ Thornton
4 *Escape* ___ with Stallone and Schwarzenegger
8 *The Big Bang Theory*'s Parsons
11 *The Young* ___ *the Restless*
12 Lightly cooked
13 Scarlett O'Hara's abode
14 Early electronics company
15 *Star Trek* ___ *Darkness*
16 "Amazing Grace" is one
17 Superstar R&B singer
19 Minnelli and Weil
20 Rapper-actor Vanilla ___
21 Nemo's weakened appendage
22 "Hello" singer
25 Texas birthplace of 17 Across
29 *Why* ___ *I Get Married?*
30 "___ the ramparts we watched…"
31 Football coach Parseghian
32 ___'s Child (former pop-R&B group of 17 Across)

35 Hit single from 17 Across's *Lemonade* album
37 Eggs
38 The ___ Commandments
39 Lena or Marilyn
42 Hit 2016 single by 17 Across
46 Nivea hit
47 Melissa George stars in *Heart* ___
48 Author LeShan
49 Tyler and Ullmann
50 "Hurting ___ Other" by the Carpenters
51 ___ *Bud* (film about a hoopster dog)
52 Kiki or Sandra
53 *One* ___ *Hill*
54 Singer Lana Del ___

DOWN

1 Fishhook prong
2 Stevie Wonder's "For ___ in My Life"

3 17 Across's second solo album
4 William, Harry or George, e.g.
5 Judge ___ Ito
6 Comedian Johnson
7 Keanu's *Matrix* films role
8 17 Across's rapper-entrepreneur spouse (wd. and ltr.)
9 ___ *la Douce*
10 *Pirates of the Caribbean: Dead* ___ *Chest*
13 Dilutes
18 *Lorenzo's* ___ with Susan Sarandon
19 Actress Lucy ___
21 *V* ___ *Vendetta* with Natalie Portman
22 The Beach Boys' "___ Some Music to Your Day"
23 *A Million Ways to* ___ *in the West*
24 Sheeran and Skrein
25 "___ Jude"
26 "___ Top" (Alabama hit)
27 Bobby ___ (hockey luminary)
28 Negative vote

30 Matthew Broderick's *Out* ___ *Limb* (2 wds.)
33 Goldwyn and Shalhoub
34 "To All the Girls ___ Loved Before"
35 Simple Minds' "___ Lights" (2 wds.)
36 ___ *for the Money* with Katherine Heigl
38 Country singer Adkins
39 "___ Up" by 17 Across
40 Merle Haggard's "___ from Muskogee"
41 Large electronic-dance-music party
42 ___ *and Loathing in Las Vegas*
43 Channing Tatum's ___ *John*
44 *Garfield* dog
45 Singer ___ J. Blige
47 *Being Mary Jane* network

Answers on page **121**

21 ACROSS

Movie Marvel

ACROSS

1 Justin Timberlake hit "___ Stop the Feeling"
5 21 Across stars in ___ Schumer's *Trainwreck*
8 *Ghosts of Girlfriends* ___
12 Baseball's Matty ___
13 Lana Del Rey, ___ Elizabeth Grant
14 R&B singer James
15 Roseanne ___
16 Carole King's "___ Too Late"
17 MGM lion Leo's sound
18 ___ King Cole
20 Fashion's ___ Karan
21 Activist and Oscar winner for *Room* (2 wds.)
26 ___ David of *Curb Your Enthusiasm*
27 Christoph Waltz's "a"
28 On the ___ (fleeing)
31 Onassis, to friends
32 *Survivor* network
33 TV cook Garten
34 "For ___ a Jolly Good Fellow"
35 TV's ___ *Flash*
36 Hanks, Baker and Atkins
38 Oscar winner for *Fences* (2 wds.)
40 American singing and rock great Joplin
43 Angela Merkel's nation (abbr.)
44 Junior's "Mama ___ to Say"
45 Rob Lowe series *The Lyon's* ___
47 *The Gambler* with ___ Wahlberg and 21 Across
51 *Bad Moms'* Kunis
52 *Transformers: ___ of Extinction*
53 Garfield frenemy
54 Cast a ___ over (worsen)
55 *The Spectacular* ___ with 21 Across
56 *McHale's* ___

DOWN

1 "The Hi De Ho Man" Calloway
2 Robin Roberts's home state, for short
3 Neither here ___ there
4 Tina, Ted or Kathleen
5 Ekberg or O'Day
6 *Dumb and Dumberer: When Harry ___ Lloyd*
7 ___, *Dear* (sitcom)
8 Eva ___ (*Evita* subject)
9 Weigh ___ (be heavy; 2 wds.)
10 Eminem hit featuring Dido
11 *United States of* ___ costars 21 Across
19 Gymnast Raisman
20 Joseph Gordon-Levitt's *Jon* features 21 Across
21 "Blah Blah ___" by Kesha
22 "So ___" (Jimmy Dorsey hit)
23 Author Murdoch biopic starring Judi Dench
24 *How to Be Single's* Wilson
25 Julia Roberts, to Eric Roberts
28 Actor Schreiber
29 Opposed to
30 Joel Edgerton of *Black* ___
32 Comic-actress Margaret ___
35 "My country, '___ of thee . . .'"
36 Lineup after B
37 Mark ___ of *NCIS*
38 Author-playwright Gore ___
39 39th U.S. Vice President Spiro ___
40 *21 ___ Street* with 21 Across
41 "Don't Cry" band
42 Jodie Foster drama
45 ___ *in Real Life*
46 Self-esteem
48 Blake Shelton's hometown: ___, Okla.
49 Swanee of song, for short
50 ___ & Peele

Answers on page **121**

27 ACROSS

Late-Night Host

ACROSS

1 North Korea's Kim ___-un
5 Money dispenser (abbr.)
8 ___ Tolkien (favorite author of 27 Across; inits.)
11 Off-Broadway award
12 *The Daily* ___ (one of 27 Across's previous TV jobs)
14 Winning tic-tac-toe crossing
15 El ___ (Weather Channel topic)
16 Corned beef ___
17 *Jeopardy!* "question" (abbr.)
18 Cheer for a team
20 Singer ___.Arie
22 *The Dark* ___ *Rises*
25 "Is ___ Crime?" (Sade hit; 2 wds.)
26 ___ Drive, Beverly Hills
27 With 34 Across, host of *The Late Show*
31 Yoko ___
32 In the past

33 "Evil Woman" band, for short
34 See 27 Across
37 John Travolta's *Get Shorty* role
39 Homer's father on *The Simpsons*
40 ___ Flickerman (*Hunger Games* character satirized by 27 Across)
41 *House of* ___ (Netflix series in which 27 Across played himself)
44 Scully on *The X-Files*
45 George Gershwin's brother
46 Barbara of *I Dream of Jeannie*
48 *Mr. Robot* star Malek
52 Nervous reaction
53 "All You ___ Is Love"
54 Actor LaBeouf
55 "Woo-hoo!"
56 2015 Melissa McCarthy comedy
57 Make money

DOWN

1 Stewart, who hosted 12 Across
2 *Star Trek: Discovery*'s Chris ___
3 *Henry & June* character Anaïs
4 ___ Clooney (27 Across's first *Late Show* guest)
5 ___ *in the Dark* (2 wds.)
6 *He's Just Not* ___ *into You*
7 Rapper ___ Def
8 *The Grapes of Wrath* family name
9 Rice-a-___
10 Civil rights hero Parks
13 ___ House Correspondents' Dinner (event hosted by 27 Across in 2006)
19 Cry of surprise
21 Afternoon snooze
22 Burger tycoon Ray
23 Taboo
24 *American* ___
25 O.J. trial judge
27 ___ *Pepper's Lonely Hearts Club Band*

28 "We have met the enemy, and ___ us" (2 wds.)
29 Singer Fitzgerald
30 Film ___
32 "___ You Lonesome Tonight?"
35 *Breaking* ___
36 *Beverly Hillbillies* star Buddy
37 27 Across book *I Am America (And So* ___ *You!)*
38 *Six Feet Under* vehicle
40 *Strangers with* ___ (sitcom 27 Across wrote for)
41 *The Second* ___ (improv group 27 Across appeared with)
42 Diva's solo
43 Naughty
44 "Rolling in the ___"
47 ___ Moines
49 Cry of surprise
50 Russian space station
51 Actor McShane

Answers on page **121**

31 ACROSS

Princess of Pop

ACROSS

1 *The* ___ *Locker*
5 Sound booster at a concert, briefly
8 An ___ effort (2 wds.)
12 Tweety line: "... ___ a puddy tat" (2 wds.)
13 ___ Paolo
14 Type of vision for Superman (hyph.)
15 Uniformed bad guys in *Raiders of the Lost Ark*
16 MTV documentary series since 1998 (2 wds.)
18 Simon Cowell show on which 31 Across was once a judge (3 wds.)
20 ___ Star Pictures
21 Nick of *Warrior*
25 Toward the back, for Captain Ahab
28 31 Across's "Where ___ You Now"
30 Bean used in Asian sauces (the four-letter spelling)
31 Singer who sold 37 million albums before her 20th birthday (2 wds.)
35 U2's frontman
36 Flapping "wing" for Dumbo
37 ___ King Cole
38 *James Bond,* ___ *007*
40 Joan's *Mad Men* hair color
42 31 Across's rap collaborator on "Pretty Girls" (2 wds.)
48 "This film has been modified from its ___ version. It has been formatted to fit your screen."
51 *Dawn of the* ___
52 Remini of *The King of Queens*
53 Quaff for Friar Tuck
54 Mark Knopfler's ___ Straits
55 31 Across's "___ Let Me Be the Last to Know"
56 Like Willie Winkie
57 Big mouths, slangily

DOWN

1 Subtle suggestion
2 State that's home to the Sundance Film Festival
3 Tear down, as a building
4 Between, in poetry
5 Fred of *Top Hat* and *Holiday Inn*
6 Jennifer Lopez's ex Anthony
7 Sulk
8 Guns n' Roses lead singer (2 wds.)
9 Abbreviation after Thurs.
10 Lummox
11 Agatha Christie's *A Pocket Full of* ___
17 Years and years and years
19 Actress Drescher
22 Bailey Bros. Building & ___ (*It's a Wonderful Life* company)
23 Model and talk show host Banks
24 *Witches of* ___ *End*
25 Agnetha, Björn, Benny and Anni-Frid's band
26 Kermit the ___
27 Pointy fork part
29 One of a purple pair for La Liz
32 *The* ___ *Show* Starring Jimmy Fallon
33 Dessert brand nobody doesn't like (2 wds.)
34 Kennedy or Reagan title, slangily
39 ___ Friday's
41 Eddie Murphy in ___ *Day Care*
43 Chew like a beaver
44 University where the Clintons met
45 Double-bunned sci-fi princess
46 Wyatt played by Kevin Costner
47 Suffix in fruity drink names
48 ___ Spice deodorant
49 ___ Speedwagon
50 McKellen of *Lord of the Rings* films

Answers on page 121

18 ACROSS

Box Office *Great*

1	2	3	4		5	6	7		8	9	10
11					12		13		14		
15					16				17		
	18			19					20		
			21				22		23		
24	25	26		27		28		29		30	31
32			33		34		35		36		
37			38		39		40		41		
		42			43		44		45		
46	47			48	49				50	51	
52			53					54			55
56			57					58			
59				60				61			

ACROSS

1 "If ___ $1,000,000 Dollars" (Barenaked Ladies hit; 2 wds.)
5 ___ *Ventura: When Nature Calls*
8 ___-la-la
11 Scarlett O'Hara's spread
12 ___-voom!
14 Comics character Alley ___
15 Actor Pickens
16 Gershwin and Levin
17 One of the Three Stooges
18 With 48 Across, star of *The Great Gatsby*
20 ___ *Pinafore*
21 *The* ___ (Sandra Bullock thriller)
22 "A Day Without Rain" singer
24 Reese Witherspoon-Matthew McConaughey movie
27 Stir-fry pan
29 Aladdin character voiced by Robin Williams
32 *Resurrection* actor Epps
34 "You dirty ___!"
36 "I've Got You Under My ___"
37 Bialik of *The Big Bang Theory*
39 Hoopster Jeremy
41 Caesar or Vicious
42 "Bat out of Hell" singer Meat ___
44 Kids' game
46 Shock and ___
48 See 18 Across
52 ___ *Deal* (1986 Schwarzenegger movie)
53 Robin Thicke's father
54 Barking sounds
56 Actor Wallach
57 Garr or Hatcher
58 *Rich Man, ___ Man*
59 Martino and Pacino
60 "Hold on a ___!"
61 Italian automaker Ferrari

DOWN

1 ___ *Always Sunny in Philadelphia*
2 ___ & Oates
3 Singer India.___
4 18 Across's *The Departed* costar Matt
5 *The* ___ (movie in which 18 Across played Howard Hughes)
6 Singer Vikki
7 Give the slip
8 18 Across's *Catch Me If You Can* costar (2 wds.)
9 *Marvin's* ___ (movie starring 18 Across)
10 *Planet of the* ___
13 ___ *of Ice and Fire* (book series on which *Game of Thrones* is based; 2 wds.)
19 *Gangs of* ___ *York* (movie starring 18 Across)
23 Affirmative answer
24 Jada Pinkett Smith, to Jaden Smith
25 Actress Thurman
26 Daniel who costarred with 18 Across in 19 Down (2 wds.)
28 Actor Penn of the *Harold & Kumar* movies
30 *The Hangover Part* ___
31 *Howards* ___
33 *Flying Down to* ___
35 Hit starring 18 Across and Kate Winslet
38 Angry with (2 wds.)
40 Afternoon snooze
43 *Two and a Half* ___
45 *What's Eating Gilbert* ___ (Johnny Depp movie costarring 18 Across)
46 Length x width
47 *The Wolf of* ___ *Street* (movie starring 18 Across)
49 *The* ___ *Bears Movie*
50 *The Man in the* ___ *Mask* (movie starring 18 Across)
51 *The Wizard* ___ (2 wds.)
55 Sign of a hit on Broadway (abbr.)

Answers on page 121

15 ACROSS

'Happy' Hitmaker

ACROSS

1 Colin Farrell-Russell Crowe drama *Winter's* ___
5 Yoko ___
8 Con game
12 "Heat of the Moment" rock band
13 Rapper-actor Bow ___
14 "___ Get It Bae" (hit single by 18 Across)
15 Singer-rapper judge on *The Voice*
17 Lena ___ of *Welcome to Sweden*
18 Shakespeare's "always"
19 Bambi's cinematic aunt
20 *The* ___ *Squad*
21 *Treasure Island* author's monogram
22 *Despicable Me* song by 15 Across
24 Billy Currington's "___ Yourself"
27 VP Biden, for short
28 ___ Zeppelin

30 Tom Hanks's *Extremely* ___ *& Incredibly Close*
31 15 Across cowrote Daft Punk's "___ Lucky"
32 Clint Eastwood's ___ *Rider*
33 Muppets Johnny Fiama and ___ Minella
34 *Inside* ___
35 Crystal ___ (singer with 20 No. 1 country hits)
36 *Beverly* ___ *Cop*
38 German filmmaker Wenders
39 Lend a hand
40 Deface
41 *The Game* network
44 Sean ___ of *The Gunman*
46 Last name of 15 Across
48 U.S. Secretary of Education Duncan (till December 2015)
49 Tolkien's talking tree
50 Legendary soprano Gluck
51 Michele and Thompson
52 Harris and Helms
53 "When I'm Not ___ the Girl I Love"

DOWN

1 Record a TV show
2 Tennis legend Arthur ___
3 Frankie Muniz comedy *Big Fat* ___
4 One of Mr. Spock's unique features
5 Clive and Jake
6 Pitcher Aaron ___
7 *The* ___ *and the Pussycat*
8 Scarlett Johansson rom-com
9 Chris Martin's band
10 Nico & Vinz hit "___ Wrong" (2 wds.)
11 ___ *in Black*
16 Jason Mraz's "You Can ___ on Me"
20 *The DUFF* with ___ Whitman
21 Rocker Stewart
22 *Wet* ___ *American Summer: First Day of Camp*
23 Billy Idol's "Rebel ___"
24 Linksman Ernie ___

25 *The Daily Show with Trevor* ___
26 *The Good Wife* star Margulies
27 Martial-arts star ___ Li
29 Kiki or Ruby ___
31 Astronaut Grissom
32 Actress Grier
34 ___ *Dogs* with John Travolta
35 15 Across's second album
37 15 Across cowrote chart-topper "Blurred ___"
38 Whitman and Disney
40 *In My* ___ (15 Across's first solo album)
41 Actor Christian ___
42 *Aloha* star Stone
43 Peter the Great, e.g.
44 Film musical ___ *Joey*
45 Tennyson's "before"
46 "In the ___ Small Hours of the Morning"
47 Actor McKellen

Answers on page **121**

15 ACROSS

Martian Man

ACROSS

1 Robert Redford's
  The Company You ___
5 Wood-shaping tool
9 *The Monuments* ___ stars
  15 Across
12 ___ *Mad, Mad, Mad, Mad*
  World (2 wds.)
13 Othello, known as
  the ___ of Venice
14 Radio's *This American*
  Life host Glass
15 *Jason Bourne* star (2 wds.)
17 Spike TV's ___ *Sync Battle*
18 Itzhak Perlman's ___ Aviv
19 Actor Jeremy ___
21 Actress Foster (*Elysium*
  costar of 15 Across)
24 Length x width ___
26 Baba of *Forty Thieves* fame
27 *Love & Mercy* star Paul ___
29 *Black* ___ *Down*
33 "___ to Pieces" by
  Del Shannon (2 wds.)

34 Baseball great Rusty ___
36 TV's *Uncle Buck*
  actress Long
37 *Promised* ___ stars
  15 Across
39 Jackson or Puente
40 *Game of Thrones*
  star Harington
41 Schumer and Poehler
43 Hitchcock's ___ *Fright*
45 Diva Ross
48 Early record company ___
  Victor
49 *Bridget Jones's Baby*
  is a ___-com
50 *War Dogs* star (2 wds.)
56 Producer-rocker Brian ___
57 Relatives of Paul Bunyan's
  helpmate Babe
58 Garfield frenemy
59 Four *Scream* films director
  Craven
60 *Mad Max: Fury* ___
61 *MacGyver* star
  George ___

DOWN

1 Actress Cattrall
2 Seventh Greek letter
3 Boston's time zone (inits.)
4 LuPone or LaBelle
5 ___ *of the Jungle*
6 Actor DeLuise
7 *We Bought a* ___ stars 15 Across
8 Linksman Els
9 *This Is Us* with
  ___ Ventimiglia
10 *Dancing with the Stars* cohost
  Andrews
11 Copies Rip Van Winkle
16 Adam Sandler's *Mr.* ___
20 Olympics sound
21 Tyler Perry's *Madea Goes to* ___
22 Russian actress
  Fonda of *Agent X*
23 "Encore un soir"
  by Celine ___
24 Novelist-diarist Nin
25 Overwhelming defeat
28 Johnnie Cochran is one (abbr.)

30 Singer-tunesmith
  Paul ___
31 Kristen ___ (15 Across's
  The Martian costar)
32 *Contagion* with ___ Winslet
  and 15 Across
35 Hieronymus ___
38 ___ *in Real Life*
42 TV's ___ *Crimes*
44 California-Nevada border lake
45 Actress-producer Barrymore
46 Actress Skye
47 Singer Tori ___
48 Author-philosopher Ayn ___
51 Tic-tac-toe loser
52 Teachers org. inits.
53 *High Sierra* star Lupino
54 Flip one's ___
  (lose self-control)
55 Hugh Jackman stars
  in ___ *Misérables*

Answers on page 121

25 ACROSS

Grammy Goddess

ACROSS

1 Fruit-filled pastries
5 Yoko ___
8 Kanye ___ ("FourFiveSeconds" with Paul McCartney & 25 Across)
12 Eric ___ of *Monty Python's Flying Circus*
13 ___ Jam (record label of 25 Across)
14 *The Thin Man* pooch
15 "Don't ___ Me"
16 Internationally banned pesticide (inits.)
17 Animal's den
18 ___ of Chucky
20 "Can't Remember to Forget You" singer with 25 Across
22 Actress Long of *The Single Moms Club*
24 Direction opposite west-southwest (inits.)
25 Nine-time Grammy-winning singing superstar
29 I ___ of Jeannie
33 "Back in the ___" (inits.)
34 Actor Daly
36 The ___ of Innocence
37 The Treasure of the Sierra ___
40 ___ Abbey
43 This Is the ___ (comedy featuring 25 Across)
45 "Kisses Don't ___" by 25 Across
46 *Grey's Anatomy* actor Patrick ___
50 *Girls* star Dunham
53 *Deliver Us from ___*
54 "Take a ___" by 25 Across
56 Han ___ (Harrison Ford *Star Wars* role)
58 *Ultraviolence* singer Del Rey
59 Actress McClanahan
60 "___ Girl (in the World)" by 25 Across
61 *Brooklyn Nine-Nine* star Samberg
62 Singer Garfunkel
63 Pop-rocker Diamond

DOWN

1 "The ___ and the Pendulum"
2 *The ___ of March*
3 *Maleficent* star Fanning
4 Actress-singer ___ Gomez
5 *The ___ Couple*
6 Actor Beatty and author Buntline
7 *Music ___ Sun* (debut album of 25 Across; 2 wds.)
8 Paul ___ of *Furious 7*
9 Actor Morales of *Playin' for Love*
10 ___ *Crazy* (Gene Wilder-Richard Pryor comedy)
11 Actress Reid
19 *Gunga ___*
21 "Shut Up ___ Drive" by 25 Across
23 Picnic pest
25 "Hot Buttered ___"
26 "The Lady ___ Tramp" (2 wds.)
27 It ___ to Be You
28 First-___ kit
30 Have a meal
31 "All Those Years ___" by George Harrison
32 *X-___: First Class*
35 *Anesthesia* star Gretchen ___
38 "Pon de ___" (first hit for 25 Across)
39 Junior commissioned naval officer (abbr.)
41 Actor Wheaton of *The Big Bang Theory*
42 Liam ___, costar of 25 Across in *Battleship*
44 Actress Messing
46 Alana ___ Garza of *Forever* (2 wds.)
47 Actor Handler
48 "Georgia on My ___"
49 *How to Train ___ Dragon*
51 ___ *Higher* by Lil Wayne
52 "___ Wanna Do" by Sheryl Crow (2 wds.)
55 *Slippery When ___* by Bon Jovi
57 Popeye's Olive ___

Answers on page **122**

17 ACROSS

Movie Royalty

ACROSS

1 *Mr. Smith ___ to Washington*
5 *A ___ in the Dark* (movie starring 17 Across)
8 *___-Devil* (movie starring 17 Across)
11 Singer Guthrie
12 *___ Haw*
13 Backyard storage
14 *The ___ Hunter* (movie featuring 17 Across)
15 Asner and Begley
16 "___ It Against Me" (Britney Spears song)
17 Three-time Oscar-winning actress (2 wds.)
20 Calls from Rocky
21 Rowboat rower
22 1988 remake of a 1950 film noir
25 *Scream* director Craven
27 *The Devil Wears ___* (movie starring 17 Across)
31 *Black Swan* star Kunis
33 Gasteyer of *Mean Girls*

35 *The ___ Lady* (biopic starring 17 Across)
36 17 Across's *The Bridges of Madison County* costar Eastwood
38 *The ___ Couple*
40 17 Across's *Julie & Julia* costar Adams
41 1998 TV movie starring Angelina Jolie
43 *___ of Africa* (movie starring 17 Across)
45 17 Across's *It's Complicated* costar (2 wds.)
50 Israeli airline (2 wds.)
51 *___ That Jazz*
52 *___ Leaf* (Walter Matthau movie; 2 wds.)
54 Phyllis's never-seen TV husband
55 *Madam Secretary* star Leoni
56 "Takin' ___ the Streets" (2 wds.)
57 *Mamma ___!* (movie starring 17 Across)

58 *Death Becomes ___* (movie starring 17 Across)
59 Frosty's is a button

DOWN

1 Josh ___ who voiced Olaf in *Frozen*
2 Utah city
3 "Waiting for the Robert ___"
4 Justin Bieber or Beyoncé title
5 *___ Lately* (former E! talk show)
6 Warren Beatty and Diane Keaton movie
7 *Say ___ the Dress* (2 wds.)
8 "There was an old woman who lived in a ___"
9 1965 Beatles song or movie
10 *Grease's* ___ Byrnes
13 Shepherd of *The View*
18 "That hurts!"
19 Jay Z's kind of music
22 Hip-hop's Run-___
23 Source of Jed Clampett's wealth

24 Boxer Laila ___
26 ___-Cat (winter vehicle)
28 Notre Dame coach Parseghian
29 *Fatso* star DeLuise
30 *___ Which Way You Can*
32 *___ in America* (TV miniseries starring 17 Across)
34 "A dillar, ___..." (2 wds.)
37 *___ Tac Dough*
39 Firecracker that fizzles
42 Take ___ (lose big; 2 wds.)
44 *Huckleberry Finn* creator Mark ___
45 Jai ___
46 *60 Minutes* correspondent Logan
47 Away from the wind
48 *___ the Woods* (movie starring 17 Across)
49 Brooklyn hoopsters
50 *A Nightmare on ___ Street*
53 "___ is me!"

Answers on page **122**

15 ACROSS

Model Citizen

ACROSS

1 *The Martial ___ Kid*
5 High-five sound
9 "Touch the ___"
12 Actress Remini
13 Ireland, in Irish
14 Actress Leoni
15 Stunning and talented fashion idol (2 wds.)
17 *Million Dollar ___* (Jon Hamm baseball movie)
18 Barbie's boyfriend
19 Actor Colfer of *Glee* (featuring 15 Across)
21 *America's Next Top ___* (starring 15 Across)
24 Actor LaBeouf
26 "___ Believer" by Neil Diamond (2 wds.)
27 "___ Smile Be Your Umbrella" (2 wds.)
29 *The Greatest Story Ever ___*
33 Singer ___ King Cole
34 James ___ of *The Fresh Prince*
of Bel-Air (featuring 15 Across)
36 ___ Howard of the Three Stooges
37 Actress de Matteo of *The Sopranos*
39 Singer India.___
40 Actress Longoria
41 Actor Badgley of *Gossip Girl* (featuring 15 Across)
43 *Lou Grant* actor Ed ___
45 Actor Leto
48 Nicole ___ Parker of *Soul Food* (featuring 15 Across)
49 "Who ___ (What's My Name)?" by Snoop Dogg (2 wds.)
50 Star of *The Fresh Prince of Bel-Air* (featuring 15 Across; 2 wds.)
56 Actor Aykroyd
57 "West Coast ___"
58 Eric ___ of *Deliver Us from Evil*
59 *Brokeback Mountain* director Lee
60 Midday
61 Tiny picnic pests

DOWN

1 Model Carol ___
2 Singer Lana Del ___
3 Sticky black-road goo
4 ___ *It Up!* (featuring 15 Across)
5 Actor Penn
6 Maya ___ (sculptor and architect)
7 *Raiders of the Lost ___*
8 Actor Joe ___
9 ___ *Wars*
10 Actress Russell of *Felicity* (featuring 15 Across)
11 Commonly mistaken for sweet potatoes
16 Actress Thorne of 4 Down (featuring 15 Across)
20 *The Cat in the ___*
21 *A Beautiful ___*
22 Actor Epps of *Higher Learning* (costarring 15 Across)
23 ___ *Night* (Tina Fey-Steve Carell comedy)
24 Shock-jock Howard ___
25 Mata ___ (World War I spy)
28 Actress Rachel Wood
30 Forewarning
31 ___ *Stinks* (starring Jason Bateman and 15 Across)
32 "___ Prudence" by the Beatles
35 *12 ___ a Slave*
38 *Tarzan, the ___ Man*
42 *The Mystery of ___ Drood*
44 *The Lion King's* royal cub
45 Actress Pinkett Smith
46 "When I Grow Up (to Be ___)" by the Beach Boys (2 wds.)
47 "___ of Fire"
48 Country singer Jackson
51 Wedding vow (2 wds.)
52 DiCaprio's nickname
53 *Pretty Little Liars'* ___ Harding
54 Network of *Rizzoli & Isles*
55 "Everything ___ Changed" by Taylor Swift

Answers on page **122**

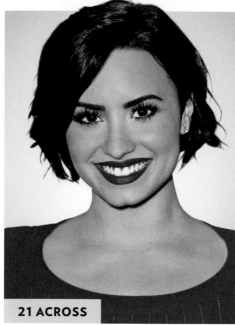

21 ACROSS

Vocal 'Dynamite'

ACROSS

1 Muhammad ___
4 *So You Think You ___ Dance*
7 ___ *Rock* stars 21 Across
11 21 Across's "___Your Heart a Break"
13 ___ *You Here* with Zach Galifianakis
14 Soprano Mills
15 Knievel the daredevil
16 Rapper-actor Vanilla ___
17 Actor Mark ___-Baker
18 Pop-rap duo of *The Bright Side* album
20 Priscilla's pilgrim John ___
21 "Really Don't Care" pop singer and actress (2 wds.)
26 Track-and-field legend Jesse ___
27 Neil Diamond's "___ Believer" (2 wds.)
28 *NCIS: ___ Angeles*
31 TV personality Leakes
32 Liam Neeson's *Rob ___*

33 ___ *We Go Again* (21 Across's No. 1 album)
34 "The ___ La La Song"
35 "For Me and My ___"
36 Tolstoy's *War and ___*
37 Creator-writer-star of *Girls* (2 wds.)
39 Actor Williams of *Chicago Fire*
42 ___ *Complicated*
43 *PBS NewsHour's* Sreenivasan
44 *The Slap* star Thurman
46 *Garfield* pooch
50 Aretha Franklin's "___ Gal Blues"
51 Robert De Niro action-drama *The ___*
52 "___ Lights" (hit single by 21 Across)
53 ___: *Warrior Princess*
54 Zac Efron's *The Lucky ___*
55 *Citizen Kane's* rose___

DOWN

1 *Ice ___: Continental Drift*

2 Steven Tyler's daughter
3 David Bowie hit "___ Been Waiting for You"
4 Woody Allen's *The Purple Rose of ___*
5 Joan of ___
6 Iggy Azalea, ___ Amethyst Amelia Kelly
7 Yo-Yo Ma's instrument
8 Dry; parched
9 *Yours, ___ & Ours*
10 *The Gunman* star Sean ___
12 *Seinfeld* girl
19 Ernie ___ (golf great)
20 "One Piece ___ Time" by Johnny Cash (2 wds.)
21 ___ *Forget* (21 Across's debut album)
22 Jug
23 Actress Suvari
24 *How to Get Away with Murder* star Davis
25 Adams or Brenneman
28 Jacob's wife
29 Killer-whale movie

30 "You Don't ___ to Miss Me" by Patty Loveless
32 Kurosawa film epic
33 The Muppets creator Jim ___
35 ___ *Shorty*
36 "___ on a Happy Face"
37 Boxing daughter of 1 Across
38 Lane or Keaton
39 21 Across was a judge of ___ *Factor* (wd. and ltr.)
40 Enthuse
41 *Dancing with the Stars'* Andrews
44 Flying saucer (inits.)
45 ___ *of Steel* with Henry Cavill
47 Novelist Caletti
48 Country singer Jimmy Dean's 1976 hit
49 *House at the ___ of the Street* starring Jennifer Lawrence

Answers on page **122**

18 ACROSS

Music Man

ACROSS

1 Jamaican music genre
4 Jim Carrey in The ___
8 Bearded farm animal that's a dino's lunch in *Jurassic Park*
12 18 Across's "Long ___ Summer"
13 Alicia Keys's voice
14 18 Across's "___ You Can Love Me This Way"
15 Carney or Garfunkel
16 Dolly Parton's "___ of Many Colors"
17 Brooklyn's NBA team
18 Nicole Kidman's singing hubby (2 wds.)
21 John Legend's "___ Day Gets Better"
22 Letterman and Matthews
26 Where 4 and 20 blackbirds were baked (3 wds.)
31 Nickname for President Truman's successor
32 Female *American Idol* judge alongside 18 Across (2 wds.)
36 Bruno Mars's "Just the Way You ___"
37 Rubber end of a pencil
38 David Copperfield's field
40 First-aid gel
44 Island neighbor of Australia, where 18 Across was born (2 wds.)
49 18 Across's "You Look ___ in My Shirt"
52 Snakelike swimmers in *The Princess Bride* and *The Deep*
53 Pester, as a spouse might
54 Car with a four-ring logo
55 Leaf-collecting tool
56 Organization for Jason Bourne (abbr.)
57 Leaning Tower city
58 Anna's *Frozen* sister, voiced by Idina Menzel
59 Make a mistake

DOWN

1 "___, Rattle and Roll"
2 *M*A*S*H* setting
3 Third floor, such as in *Home Alone*
4 ___ 1 (sound barrier in *The Right Stuff*)
5 Baseball's Matty
6 Common movie-rating symbol
7 Hoda of morning TV
8 18 Across's "You ___ Fly"
9 Katherine Heigl's ___ for the Money
10 ___-rock (music genre, briefly)
11 Pennington and Cobb
19 The ___ Man (classic comedy-mystery film)
20 "19" and "21" singer
23 One with a backstage concert pass (abbr.)
24 ___ out a living
25 Speaks, informally
27 Emma Roberts, to Julia Roberts
28 *The Lion King* continent (abbr.)
29 Popeye baby Swee'___
30 Nickname for the WWE's wrestling taxman Irwin R. Schyster
32 *Space ___* (with Michael Jordan)
33 Time in history
34 Less than zero (abbr.)
35 Type of hygiene or thermometer
39 *Slumdog Millionaire* country
41 Bass or Armstrong
42 Radio-station studio sign (2 wds.)
43 ___ Allan Poe
45 18 Across duet "We ___ Us"
46 Enthusiasm
47 Lodge members named for antlered animals
48 In the Atlantic
49 Alfred E. Neuman's ___-toothed grin
50 Yes, in Paris
51 Pigs out, for short

Answers on page 122

18 ACROSS

Interstellar Star

ACROSS

1 Muhammad and Laila
5 Mont Blanc is one
8 Iowa State University's town
12 *The ___ Knight Rises* stars 18 Across
13 Rapper ___ Wayne
14 Actress Carter
15 Jai ___
16 *Little Women* author's monogram
17 Les Paul and Mary Ford standard
18 Star of *The Intern* and *Interstellar* (2 wds.)
21 Minnesota-to-Arkansas direction
22 *Damn Yankees'* Hunter
23 Gold, to Sofia Vergara
26 *Who Do You Think You ___?* (genealogy series)
28 *The ___ Wears Prada* stars 18 Across
32 *Bride ___* with Kate Hudson and 18 Across
34 *House at the ___ of the Street*
36 Jake Gyllenhaal and 18 Across star in ___ *& Other Drugs*
37 *Lifestyles of the Rich and Famous* with Robin ___
39 American Pharoah's feedbag morsel
41 *Orange Is the ___ Black*
42 Ooh and ___ (enthuse)
44 *Leaving ___ Vegas*
46 A star of *Spotlight* and the *Hunger Games* films (2 wds.)
52 *Where the ___ Things Are*
53 Sea god of Irish myth
54 "Jingle Bell Rock" duo ___ & Oates
56 *Two ___ Half Men* (2 wds.)
57 *The Duff* star Whitman
58 Eminem movie *8 ___*
59 Shaquille O'___
60 Sandra Bullock's *Gun ___*
61 Sarah Michelle Gellar TV series *The Crazy ___*

DOWN

1 Computing pioneer Lovelace
2 "___ Land" by Demi Lovato (2 wds.)
3 Hassan Rouhani's nation
4 Pickup basketball: shirts and ___
5 "The gang's ___" (2 wds.)
6 Supermodel Adriana ___
7 Oliver ___ of *Chicago Med*
8 Poe poem "___ Lee"
9 *The Cat's ___* with Kirsten Dunst
10 ___ *Enchanted* stars 18 Across
11 Fell a dragon, e.g.
19 Conductor ___-Pekka Salonen
20 "It ___ to Be You"
23 *The ___ and the Pussycat*
24 Carly ___ Jepsen
25 "R.I.P." by Rita ___
27 Rock's Brian ___
29 Fashion's Diane ___ Furstenberg
30 "___ Got My Love to Keep Me Warm"
31 Former U.S. Treasury Secretary Jack ___
33 Kerry Washington's TV series
35 "Without Your Love" singer Roger ___
38 Actor Holbrook
40 T, to Hippocrates
43 *The Hangover* films' Ed ___
45 Reality TV's *The Joe ___ Show*
46 *Black ___* with Natalie Portman
47 Fork prong
48 *Bridge of Spies* features Alan ___
49 Neil Diamond's "Hell ___"
50 Abel's sibling
51 *Winnie ___ Pu* (Latin edition of *Winnie the Pooh*)
55 18 Across won an Oscar for ___ *Misérables*

Answers on page **122**

18 ACROS

Panther Power

ACROSS

1 Actors Harris and Helms
4 "For Sale" and "Help Wanted" notices
7 *The Bell* ___
10 "One Day in ___ Life" by Michael Jackson
12 Actor Wyle of *The Librarians*
14 *Still the Same* ___ *Me* by George Jones
15 Actress Fanning
16 Opera song
17 Egg-laying chicken
18 *12 Years a Slave* Oscar actress (2 wds.)
21 Yoko ___
22 Actress Leoni
23 Comedian Caesar or punk rocker Vicious
26 Actress Poehler
28 Director McQueen of *12 Years a Slave* (starring 18 Across)
32 Actor Kinnear
34 *Are We There* ___*?*
36 "___ Sagan"
37 Actor Killam of *12 Years a Slave* (starring 18 Across)
39 ___ Na Na
41 24-7 movie channel (inits.)
42 *V for Vendetta* actor Stephen ___
44 Actor Torn of *Men in Black 3*
46 Mistress Shaw in *12 Years a Slave* (2 wds.)
52 Actress Long of *The Divide*
53 Actor Florek
54 Actor Giamatti of *12 Years a Slave* (starring 18 Across)
56 Singer Cole
57 ___ ball (common arcade game)
58 Actress Turturro
59 Emergency medical service (inits.)
60 Suffix with count, heir or lion
61 *Orange Is the* ___ *Black*

DOWN

1 *Eagle* ___ (Shia LaBeouf thriller)
2 *American* ___ *Posse* by Tori Amos
3 George Takei *Star Trek* role
4 Branch of biology
5 ___ *the Explorer*
6 "It's Hard to Be a ___ in the City"
7 Screenwriter Ridley of *12 Years a Slave* (starring 18 Across)
8 "Break ___" (good-luck wish to a performer; 2 wds.)
9 ___ *911!* (TV cop comedy)
11 ___ *Man* (sci-fi crime film starring 55 Down)
13 Sean ___ of *Will and Grace*
19 "Genie ___ Bottle" by Christina Aguilera (2 wds.)
20 ___ of Office (elected official's Inauguration promise)
23 Sergeant abbr.
24 Lyricist Gershwin
25 James Van ___ Beek
27 "___ I Can" by Sammy Davis Jr.
29 *All You Can* ___
30 Singer Damone
31 *A Nightmare on* ___ *Street*
33 Teri ___ of *Tootsie*
35 *Game of* ___
38 *Mars* ___ *Moms*
40 First ___ (help administered by 59 Across)
43 Not asleep
45 "___ Don't Preach"
46 Actress Hathaway
47 Actor Neeson of *Non-Stop* (costarring 18 Across)
48 Singer Domino
49 *The Defiant* ___
50 ___ *Man* (Dustin Hoffman Oscar film)
51 "Dump the ___"
55 Actor Jude ___

Answers on page 122

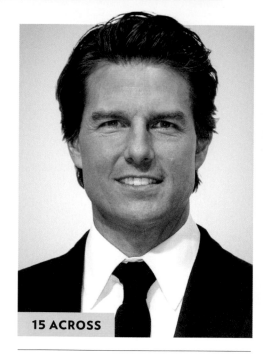

15 ACROSS

Man on a Mission

ACROSS

1 *Love the Coopers* actor Arkin
5 Cole Porter tune "I ___ Love" (2 wds.)
9 Mark Wahlberg's *The Italian* ___
12 *Frasier* actress Gilpin
13 NFL great Torretta
14 Japan's PM Shinzō ___
15 *Mission Impossible* films' star (2 wds.)
17 John Cusack's ___ *Air*
18 *Dr.* ___ with actor Jeong
19 VH1 series *Dating* ___
21 Scorpions' "___ Me, Please Me"
24 15 Across's *Collateral* costar ___ Pinkett Smith
26 ___ *of the Worlds* with 15 Across
27 Heidi Klum's ex
29 *Beavis and Butt-* ___
33 Sinatra's "___ Got the World on a String"
34 Sportscaster ___ Johnson Jr.
36 R&B quartet ___ Hill
37 "Don't Go ___ the Water"
39 "Perfect Day" musician Lou ___
40 Zeus or Neptune, e.g.
41 *The* ___ *Samurai* stars 15 Across
43 Cara, Dunne or Papas
45 *Beauty and the* ___
48 Hawaiian wreath
49 Sandra Bullock rom-com ___ *About Steve*
50 *Irrational Man* and *Birdman* star (2 wds.)
56 Zero
57 ___ *Flux* with Charlize Theron
58 Celine Dion's "___ Day Has Come" (2 wds.)
59 *Knight and* ___ with 15 Across
60 Patrick Dempsey's ___ *of Honor*
61 "Smooth Operator" singer ___

DOWN

1 Brad Renfro stars in ___ *Pupil*
2 Melissa ___ of 15 Across's *Oblivion*
3 *Million Dollar* ___ with Jon Hamm
4 Jonas and Cannon
5 Natalie Portman's *Jane Got* ___ (2 wds.)
6 Livy's 1,002
7 ___ and outs (details)
8 Documentary ___ *in Sight* (2 wds.)
9 ___ *Reacher* stars 15 Across
10 Clarinet's relative
11 ___ *It Like Beckham*
16 *Wild* star Witherspoon
20 Ooh and ___ (gush over)
21 Ashley or Mary-Kate Olsen
22 Roof rim
23 Bob Dylan's "The Times They ___ Changin'" (2 wds.)
24 Former Federal Reserve head Yellen
25 "It's a Sin to Tell ___" (2 wds.)
28 Miscalculates
30 15 Across's ___ *of Tomorrow*
31 Original spelling of Elvis Presley's middle name
32 ___, *Where's My Car?*
35 Brickell and Falco
38 Author Stevenson's monogram
42 Bradley Cooper's *The* ___ (ltr. and wd.)
44 Ora and Coolidge
45 Springsteen backers the E Street ___
46 Film mastermind Kazan
47 Disney's *Austin &* ___
48 Nathan or Diane
51 "Cry ___ River" (2 wds.)
52 *The* ___ *Squad*
53 "___ Clear Day (You Can See Forever)" (2 wds.)
54 Orlando Bloom movie ___ *Kelly*
55 Lamb's aunt

Answers on page **122**

8 ACROSS

Renaissance Man of Rap

ACROSS

1 Hitchcock's ___ *Window*
5 The Notorious ___
 ("Brooklyn's Finest"
 collaborator of 8 Across)
8 *Magna Carta … Holy Grail* rapper (wd. & init.)
12 Singer Fitzgerald
13 *New Year's* ___
14 Confederate general Robert ___ (init. & wd.)
15 Actor Morales of *Criminal Minds*
16 *The Catcher in the* ___
17 "___ Like an Eagle"
18 Blythe ___ of *Little Fockers*
20 *The Jetsons* pooch
21 R&B superstar Knowles
 (wife of 8 Across)
24 Comedian Burnett
27 21 Across fans
 (aka the ___ hive)
28 *Wheel of Fortune* vowel buy
 (wd. & ltr.)
31 "___ the Whistle" by 8 Across
32 "Say hello to the ___ guy"
 (8 Across's lyrics)
33 ___ *White and the Huntsman*
34 "7th Deadly ___" by Ice-T
 (feat. lyrics by 8 Across)
35 Actor Worthington
36 Birth name of 8 Across
 (with last name Carter)
37 Singer with 55 Across on "Run
 This Town" by 8 Across
39 The ___ & the Papas
 ('60s folk-rock group)
42 Cass ___ (lead singer of
 39 Across)
46 Clive ___ of *The Knick*
47 "Medicine ___" by Paul
 McCartney & Wings
49 Rob ___ of *Parks and Recreation*
50 Rapper Snoop ___
51 *H2O: Just* ___ *Water*
52 *The Quiet* ___ (horror film)
53 *Something* ___ by Robin Thicke
54 Rapper-actor ___ Def
55 Kanye ___ ("Who Gon Stop
 Me" collaborator of 8 Across)

DOWN

1 *Twilight's* Nikki ___
2 *Frozen* protagonist
3 *Cabaret's* Cumming
4 "Over the ___"
5 *Extant's* Halle ___
6 Blue ___ (daughter of
 8 Across & 21 Across)
7 "___ Baby Ain't I Good to You"
8 Actor Eisenberg of
 Now You See Me
9 "I Got ___ of Livin'
 to Do" (2 wds.)
10 *The 40-___-Old Virgin*
11 ___ *Dark Thirty*
19 Slithery fish
20 *American Idol* rocker ___ Young
22 President Barack ___
23 ___ *Kelly* (Heath Ledger-
 Orlando Bloom film)
24 *2 Broke Girls*
 network (inits.)
25 *Legends* actress Larter
26 Actor-director Howard
28 Actress Gasteyer
29 "It's ___ or Never"
30 *A League of Their* ___
32 "___! Humbug"
33 ___ *Hal*
35 Bro's sibling
36 Lorne Michaels's weekend
 show (inits.)
37 "Home on the ___"
38 *Revenge of the* ___
39 Brit band Depeche ___
40 Absent without leave (inits.)
41 Actresses Ryan and Tilly
43 Actress Skye of
 Return to Babylon
44 Has a debt
45 The Game's "Drug ___"
47 Def ___ (former record
 label of 8 Across)
48 *Much* ___
 About Nothing

Answers on page **122**

1. Bravo's *Real Housewives* franchise has cropped up all over the U.S. How many American locales have been featured?

A. 6   **B.** 10
C. 11   **D.** 9

2. On *The Late Late Show with James Corden,* the host invites famous guests to drive around in a car in what recurring segment?

A. Comedians in Cars Getting Coffee
B. Thank You Notes
C. Carpool Karaoke
D. Celebrities Read Mean Tweets

3. Michael Crichton, who wrote and directed the 1973 *Westworld* film, also wrote a novel that inspired which action-film franchise?

A. Indiana Jones
B. Jurassic Park
C. Mission Impossible
D. James Bond

Television Trivia
10 questions to test your small-screen knowledge

4. Which *Game of Thrones* costars wed on June 23, 2018, in Aberdeenshire, Scotland?

A. Rose Leslie and Kit Harington
B. Lena Headey and Nikolaj Coster-Waldau
C. Sophie Turner and Kit Harington
D. Gwendoline Christie and Iain Glen

5. Which member of Netflix's 2018 *Queer Eye* hit reboot cast was recruited via social media instead of submitting an application?

A. Jonathan Van Ness
B. Bobby Berk
C. Tan France
D. Karamo Brown
E. Antoni Porowski

6. Contestants have been trying to find love on ABC's *The Bachelor* for more than 20 seasons. In the show's history (not including *The Bachelorette* and spinoff shows), only one Bachelor has married the woman who received the final rose. Who is he?

A. Sean Lowe
B. Ben Higgins
C. Jason Mesnick
D. Brad Womack

7. Reed Morano, who directed the first three episodes of Hulu's *The Handmaid's Tale,* worked as a cinematographer on which singer's video album?

A. Katy Perry's *Dark Horse*
B. Taylor Swift's *Reputation*
C. Rihanna's *Unapologetic*
D. Beyoncé's *Lemonade*

8. Which *Office* star filmed the Scranton cell-phone footage that runs during the opening credits?

A. Steve Carell
B. Jenna Fischer
C. John Krasinski
D. B.J. Novak

9. After Fox canceled *Brooklyn Nine-Nine* in 2018, NBC picked up the sitcom, much to the relief of famous fans. Who was *not* one of the celebs who rallied support on the Internet for the show?

A. Benicio del Toro
B. Lin-Manuel Miranda
C. Mark Hamill
D. Seth Meyers

10. Food Network's *Beat Bobby Flay* features various chefs competing to take down Iron Chef Bobby Flay, with the help of some famous guests. Which celeb has *not* appeared on the show?

A. Bethenny Frankel
B. Blake Shelton
C. Apolo Ohno
D. Lance Bass

ANSWERS Television: 1B. 2C. 3B. 4A. 5C. 6A. 7D. 8C. 9A. 10B. **Grande:** 1C. 2B. **Royal Year:** 1C. 2B. 3A. 4A. 5A.

Wise Words
Ariana Grande: Girl Power

1. "My fellow women are definitely something that I will always be one of the first to speak up about," Ariana Grande told Carson Daly on 97.1 AMP Radio's *The Daly Download* in 2016. Which singer was she speaking out to support?

A. Selena Gomez
B. Taylor Swift
C. Kesha
D. Demi Lovato

2. "Love is a really scary thing, and you never know what's going to happen. It's one of the most beautiful things in life, but it's one of the most terrifying. It's worth the fear because you have more knowledge, experience, you learn from people, and you have memories," Grande told *Seventeen* magazine in 2013. The "No Tears Left to Cry" singer was briefly engaged to which comedian before they split?

A. Michael Che
B. Pete Davidson
C. Bo Burnham
D. Colin Jost

Royal Year!
The royals add to their ranks

1. Britain's Prince William and future Queen Kate Middleton welcomed their third child, Prince Louis Arthur Charles of Cambridge, on April 23, 2018. What time was the little prince born?

A. 12:15 p.m.
B. 11:37 a.m.
C. 11:01 a.m.
D. 10:07 a.m.

2. Prince Louis's first name honors Prince Philip's uncle Lord Louis Mountbatten, and his third name is a nod to Charles. His middle name, Arthur, refers to Victoria's third son and means what animal in Celtic?

A. Deer
B. Bear
C. Hound
D. Horse

3. Prince Harry's bride, Meghan Markle, was raised in California and became an actress. Where did the future duchess attend college?

A. Northwestern University
B. New York University
C. Boston University
D. University of South Carolina

4. Princess Diana and Prince Charles took baby William overseas 31 years before Kate and Will took George to the same country for his first official royal tour in 2014. Which country did they first visit?

A. Australia
B. Kenya
C. The United States
D. New Zealand

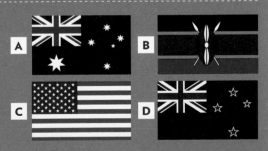

5. Which famous couple did not attend Harry and Meghan's wedding in 2018?

A. Barack and Michelle Obama
B. David and Victoria Beckham
C. George and Amal Clooney
D. Serena Williams and Alexis Ohanian

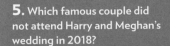

WORD SEARCH

```
L R T N S B F V G V Q Q
H L D U Y A M T O F A N
V O Z D P S V R L G O U
V L U N X K P A D L U H
L Y V A O E C I N I K E
O M G L H T F N T N M E
F P A E I B B W R S A P
Q I M V O A J R U L J H
G C I E Y L B E O A D E
E S A L P L O C C N B A
T X M C I C F K P I Z T
Z K I D R A W R O F Y E
```

```
Z C L R E N T S P N M
B G A Y L E T I H H I
M T R E B E Z O I O L
W A R O D U E N L S W P
B Z M M E Q Q I A T A N
O G A C I H C L N C U N
O N G P S A S L T E K R
K C A Y S R I I H F E
Y A Z Z U P M F R F E M
H Z I Q G O T G O E P J
P L N Z B E W S P S I G
Q N E T W O R K Y C G
```

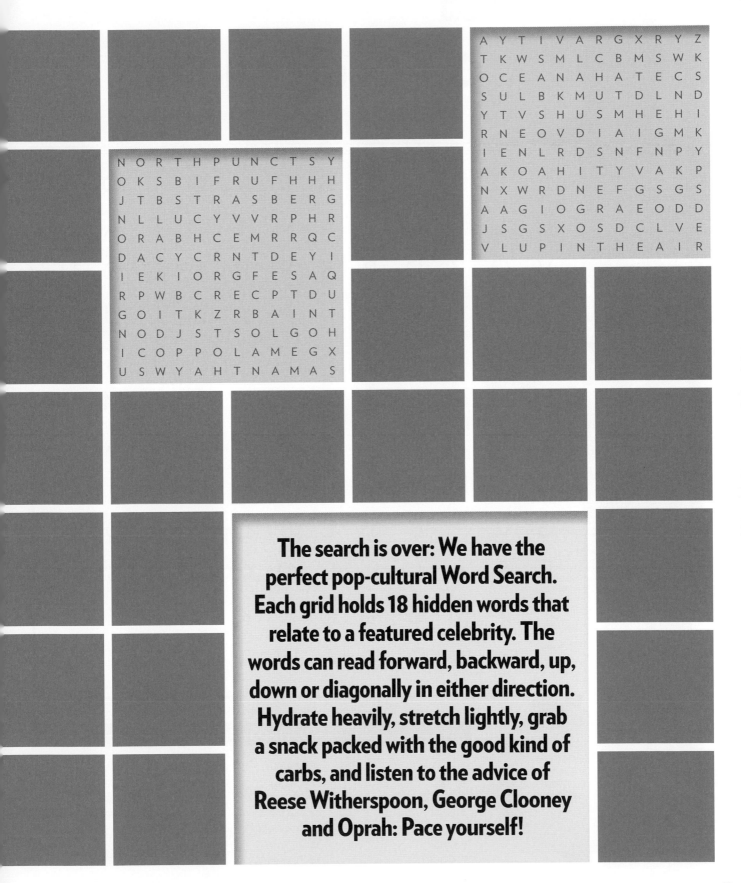

Grid 1:
```
N O R T H P U N C T S Y
O K S B I F R U F H H H
J T B S T R A S B E R G
N L L U C Y V V R P H R
O R A B H C E M R R Q C
D A C Y C R N T D E Y I
I E K I O R G F E S A Q
R P W B C R E C P T D U
G O I T K Z R B A I N T
N O D J S T S O L G O H
I C O P P O L A M E G X
U S W Y A H T N A M A S
```

Grid 2:
```
A Y T I V A R G X R Y Z
T K W S M L C B M S W K
O C E A N A H A T E C S
S U L B K M U T D L N D
Y T V S H U S M H E H I
R N E O V D I A I G M K
I E N L R D S N F N P Y
A K O A H I T Y V A K P
N X W R D N E F G S G S
A A G I O G R A E O D D
J S G S X O S D C L V E
V L U P I N T H E A I R
```

The search is over: We have the perfect pop-cultural Word Search. Each grid holds 18 hidden words that relate to a featured celebrity. The words can read forward, backward, up, down or diagonally in either direction. Hydrate heavily, stretch lightly, grab a snack packed with the good kind of carbs, and listen to the advice of Reese Witherspoon, George Clooney and Oprah: Pace yourself!

On-Court All-Star

```
L R T N S B F V G V Q Q
H L D U Y A M T O F A N
V O Z D P S V R L G O U
V L U N X K P A D L U H
L Y V A O E C I N I K E
O M G L H T F N T N M E
F P A E I B B W R S A P
Q I M V O A J R U L J H
G C I E Y L B E O A D E
E S A L P L O C C N B A
T X M C I C F K P I Z T
Z K I D R A W R O F Y E
```

LeBron James has won four NBA titles: two in Miami, one in Cleveland and one in 2020 with the Los Angeles Lakers.

FIND THESE

1 MVP
2 NBA
3 GOLD
4 HEAT
5 NIKE
6 OHIO
7 COURT

8 MIAMI
9 VOGUE
10 BRONZE
11 FINALS
12 FORWARD
13 ACTIVIST
14 OLYMPICS

15 SAVANNAH
16 CLEVELAND
17 BASKETBALL
18 TRAIN WRECK

Answers on page 123

Legal Lady

```
N E R D L I H C W G T W
Z L N S A M A B A L A J
M R Z I D R A P E R S P
A I K N L W O O D S L Y
N G G G G E M D E E T L
A E Q K Q R H R X D F L
I N D X E A T T U N O A
S O D R J C E M K O C G
I G X N A S H V I L L E
U A M J M O E T A B A L
O R S O E L K L O S C W
L D W J S C O G J T E W
```

FIND THESE

1 MUD
2 BEST
3 SING
4 TOTH
5 ARDEN
6 JAMES
7 OSCAR

8 WOODS
9 BLONDE
10 DRAPER
11 ACTRESS
12 ALABAMA
13 LEGALLY
14 CHILDREN

15 GONE GIRL
16 LOUISIANA
17 NASHVILLE
18 WALK THE LINE

Answers on page 123

An actress who has worked since age 14, Reese Witherspoon is now also a producer. Her company Hello Sunshine brought out the films *Gone Girl* and *Wild* as well as *Big Little Lies* on TV.

Dreamy Doc

A	Y	T	I	V	A	R	G	X	R	Y	Z
T	K	W	S	M	L	C	B	M	S	W	K
O	C	E	A	N	A	H	A	T	E	C	S
S	U	L	B	K	M	U	T	D	L	N	D
Y	T	V	S	H	U	S	M	H	E	H	I
R	N	E	O	V	D	I	A	I	G	M	K
I	E	N	L	R	D	S	N	F	N	P	Y
A	K	O	A	H	I	T	Y	V	A	K	P
N	X	W	R	D	N	E	F	G	S	G	S
A	A	G	I	O	G	R	A	E	O	D	D
J	S	G	S	X	O	S	D	C	L	V	E
V	L	U	P	I	N	T	H	E	A	I	R

George Clooney has starred in dozens of films. He and his wife, attorney Amal Clooney, have donated hundreds of thousands of dollars to various global causes.

FIND THESE

1 AMAL
2 ARGO
3 REDS
4 DANNY
5 OCEAN
6 AWARDS
7 BATMAN

8 TWELVE
9 ACADEMY
10 GRAVITY
11 SISTERS
12 SOLARIS
13 SPY KIDS
14 SYRIANA

15 KENTUCKY
16 ALAMUDDIN
17 LOS ANGELES
18 UP IN THE AIR

Answers on page **123**

Triple Threat

```
R V Y H S I D L I H C N
A X P E O D N A L A O J
P G I R L S S M L J M M
P S H L O N P R R W M Z
E L L E H C I M O U U I
R T B B Y S D K T O N P
V W G O S O E B C Y I Z
O D R I E W R Y A M T V
B T A I Y J M C D J Y B
N N Q A T G A M B I N O
Z Q E N H E N O B D E R
I S I N G E R R R C K L T
```

FIND THESE

1 MCDJ
2 SOLO
3 TROY
4 ACTOR
5 GIRLS
6 LANDO
7 RAPPER

8 SINGER
9 WEIRDO
10 WRITER
11 GAMBINO
12 REDBONE
13 CHILDISH
14 McKINLEY

15 MICHELLE
16 COMMUNITY
17 SPIDER-MAN
18 CALRISSIAN

Answers on page 123

The *Community* alum turns everything he touches to gold—writer, actor, singer and funnyman Donald Glover starred on the hit TV show *Atlanta* while owning summer 2018's No. 1 song, "This Is America."

Sitcom Legend

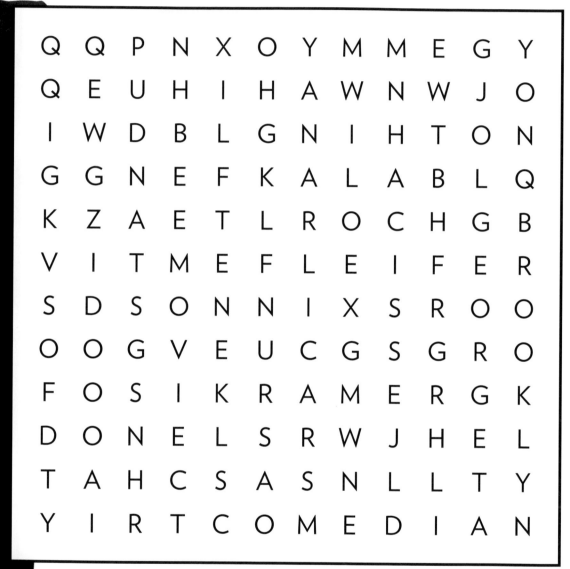

```
Q Q P N X O Y M M E G Y
Q E U H I H A W N W J O
I W D B L G N I H T O N
G G N E F K A L A B L Q
K Z A E T L R O C H G B
V I T M E F L E I F E R
S D S O N N I X S R O O
O O G V E U C G S G R O
F O S I K R A M E R G K
D O N E L S R W J H E L
T A H C S A S N L L T Y
Y I R T C O M E D I A N
```

Seinfeld is considered by many the best sitcom of all time. Jerry Seinfeld now hosts the Netflix show *Comedians in Cars Getting Coffee.*

FIND THESE

1 KAL
2 CARS
3 EMMY
4 LENO
5 ELAINE
6 GEORGE
7 KRAMER

8 LEIFER
9 OSWEGO
10 SASCHA
11 JESSICA
12 NETFLIX
13 NOTHING
14 STAND-UP

15 BEE MOVIE
16 BROOKLYN
17 COMEDIAN
18 THE GIFTED

Answers on page 123

Queen of Talk

```
Z  C  L  R  E  N  T  S  P  N  M  H
B  G  A  Y  L  E  T  I  H  H  I  I
M  T  R  E  B  E  Z  O  I  O  L  C
W  A  R  O  D  U  E  N  L  S  W  P
B  Z  M  M  E  Q  Q  I  A  T  A  N
O  G  A  C  I  H  C  L  N  C  U  N
O  N  G  P  S  A  S  L  T  E  K  R
K  C  A  Y  S  R  I  I  H  F  E  P
Y  A  Z  Z  U  P  M  F  R  F  E  M
H  Z  I  Q  G  O  T  G  O  E  P  J
P  L  N  Z  B  E  W  S  P  S  I  Q
Q  N  E  T  W  O  R  K  Y  C  G  X
```

FIND THESE

1 BOOK
2 HOST
3 SHOW
4 EBERT
5 GAYLE
6 HARPO
7 QUEEN
8 SOFIA
9 EFFECT
10 EUDORA
11 GUSSIE
12 CHICAGO
13 NETWORK
14 STEDMAN
15 ILLINOIS
16 MAGAZINE
17 MILWAUKEE
18 PHILANTHROPY

Answers on page 123

Now among the richest women in the world, Oprah Winfrey got her start as a news anchor in Baltimore.

Her *Marvel* character
(here in 2012's
The Avengers) headlines
a solo Black Widow film,
expected out in 2021.

Action Hero

```
N O R T H P U N C T S Y
O K S B I F R U F H H H
J T B S T R A S B E R G
N L L U C Y V V R P H R
O R A B H C E M R R Q C
D A C Y C R N T D E Y I
I E K I O R G F E S A Q
R P W B C R E C P T D U
G O I T K Z R B A I N T
N O D J S T S O L G O H
I C O P P O L A M E G X
U S W Y A H T N A M A S
```

FIND THESE

1 HER
2 CHEF
3 LOST
4 LUCY
5 NORTH
6 PEARL
7 SCOOP
8 DON JON
9 INGRID
10 COPPOLA
11 DE PALMA
12 FAVREAU
13 AVENGERS
14 SAMANTHA
15 HITCHCOCK
16 STRASBERG
17 BLACK WIDOW
18 THE PRESTIGE

Answers on page **123**

Scarlett Johansson joined an elite group of actors nominated for two Oscars in the same year. In 2020 she earned nods for her work in *Jojo Rabbit* and *Marriage Story*.

ARROW-WORD

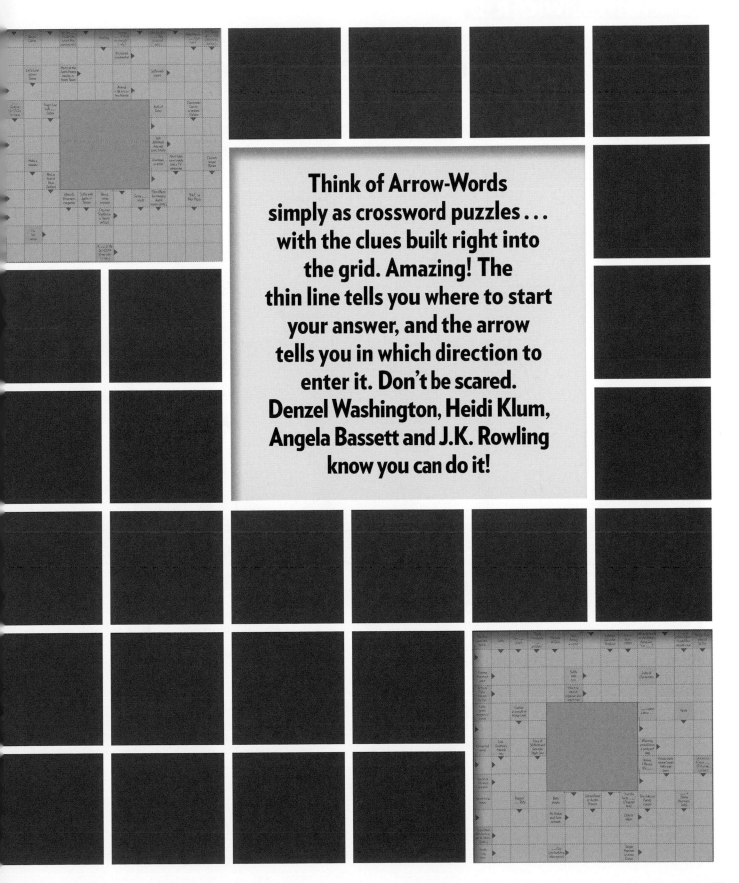

Think of Arrow-Words simply as crossword puzzles . . . with the clues built right into the grid. Amazing! The thin line tells you where to start your answer, and the arrow tells you in which direction to enter it. Don't be scared. Denzel Washington, Heidi Klum, Angela Bassett and J.K. Rowling know you can do it!

Motion-Picture Lead

Family ___ (game show)		Singer Céline		He Got ___ (Spike Lee sports film starring him)		Nothing		"Gimme ___" ("Hold on," slangily; 2 wds)		Film for him: ___ Tide (shade of red)		Katy Perry's "___ Your Love"	The Taking of ___ 123 (2009 film for him)
								It's poured on pancakes					
The ___ Brief (Grisham thriller)		La La Land actress Stone		Myers of the Austin Powers movies, or boxer Tyson						Suffix with expert			
His first name								Animal with one or two humps					
The Hollywood Walk of ___	___ Gangster (2007 film for him)		Singer Lisa "Left ___" Lopes							Kotb of Today		Funnyman Carvey or actress Delany	
April follower										'60s Southeast Asia war zone, briefly			
James Bond in Diamonds ___ Forever		Make a mistake								Unwritten, as a test	Alex Haley novel made into a TV miniseries		Country singer Rimes
			Bird or fruit of New Zealand										
Annoy				Alfred E. Neuman's magazine	Suffix with Japan or Taiwan	Blend, using a spoon		Santa ___ winds	Film effects for creating digital scenes (inits.)			"Me?," to Miss Piggy	
The "C" of C.S.I.						City near Seattle (or a Toyota pickup)							
___ Man (heist film for him)		His last name											
				A ___ in the Sun (2014 B'way play for him)									

Answers on page 123

Runway Favorite

Clues:

- America's Got ___ (TV show for her)
- Hawaiian neckwear
- Occupation that put her on magazine covers
- Darth Vader's childhood nickname
- Lagerfeld or Marx
- Gehrig or Ferrigno
- Dawber or Grier
- Her mentoring sidekick on TV (2 wds.)
- Singer Carly ___ Jepsen
- ___ Illustrated Swimsuit Issue
- ___ mater (school graduated from)
- Swiss mountain
- Tax agency with a 4/15 deadline (abbr.)
- Former CIA head Panetta
- Folded item replaced by GPS (2 wds.)
- Nat ___ (Wicked Tuna channel)
- Her first and last name
- Actress Salonga or Thompson
- Twisted-together part of a shoelace
- What a courtroom witness is under
- Tom Petty's "___ All Work Out"
- Robert of Raging Bull and Taxi Driver
- Largest U.S. tribe
- "Illmatic" rapper
- Actor and SNL alum Aykroyd
- Tennis great Arthur
- Broadway or TV offerings
- Primetime awards (she won one in 2013)
- Abbr. after Yale or Harvard
- Judge in The People v. O.J. Simpson
- Dancing with the Stars judge Goodman
- Vanilla ___ (DIY Network host)
- Performs in a movie
- Violet chews it in the Willy Wonka movies
- Genetic material (inits.)
- History Channel's The Curse of ___ Island
- Slanted, like this type
- Bride's counterpart
- Her fashion design TV series 2004-2018
- Robin Williams sitcom, The Crazy ___
- Hockey goalie face protectors

Answers on page 123

Wizarding Writer

Her full name, on books	Kevin who won an Oscar for *A Fish Called Wanda*	Stimpy's cartoon pal	Pig noises	▼	Katy Perry's "The One That Got ___"	*Letters from ___ Jima*	Flanders of Springfield or Stark of Westeros	Fill-up for the cars in *Cars*	"He who shall not be named" at Hogwarts	▼	Stan of Marvel Comics fame	Tornado centers
▶									Nashville's Grand ___ Opry	▶		
Bun-headed space princess	▶				Redheaded Ron of Gryffindor house							
▶					Binges (on), briefly				Actor Billy ___ Williams	▶		
Ron's sister at Hogwarts		Scot's cap							Thurman of *Pulp Fiction*		Like many of the extras in *Lawrence of Arabia*	
▶		▼							▶		▼	*The ___ of Secrets* (part of her 2nd book title)
Hedwig the owl and Scabbers the rat, e.g.	Gold, silver or bronze, at the Olympics		Greek goddess of wisdom						*Lord of The Rings* bad guy	▶		
▶			▼						Bit of a cheerleader's cheer	▶		
Watson who played Hermione Granger		State where the Sundance film festival is held							Not-yet-decided, on a schedule (inits.)	▶		
"How stupid of me!" sound	▶	▼		Hunchbacked helper in *Young Frankenstein*	▼	Myrna of old movies	▼	Johnny of *Pirates of the Caribbean*	Feline, such as Filch's Mrs. Norris	Set ablaze	Fail or sculpt suffix	
Consumed, as some Bertie Bott's beans	▶			High school singing group (2 wds.)	▶		▼		▼	▼	▼	
▶				Alley-___ (basketball pass)	▶			Million or billion add-on	▶			
Rickman who played Severus Snape	Hogwarts boy with a lightning bolt scar (2 wds.)	▶										

Answers on page 123

Onscreen Sensation

Her first and last name	Guts	Day-___ paint	"That's somebody ___ problem"	Michele of *Glee*	Help, during a crime		Leftover bit in the fireplace	U-turn from NNW	Wicked Witch of the West's dying line: "I'm ___!"		"___ a yellow ribbon 'round the ole oak tree"	Singer Tina, played by her
Dakota Fanning's sister					Suffix with lion				Lucy of *Elementary*			
Activist Parks, played by her					Place to munch popcorn and watch her							
Little green veggies in a pod		Captain in pursuit of Moby-Dick							"___ upon a time . . ."		Gunk	
Unwanted email	Lisa Kudrow's *Friends* role		Tracy of *30 Rock* and *Saturday Night Live*						Warning sound from a junkyard dog			
									Honey, I Shrunk the ___	Potato state where Sarah Palin was born		*American Horror ___* (TV series for her)
Game of Thrones network												
Re-mi-fa-so notes		Rapper ___ Rida		Belly laughs		James Bond or Austin Powers		"Just the facts, ___" (*Dragnet* line)	*The Addams Family* cousin		___-x (Baby boomers' kids)	
				Mr. Robot and *Suits* network					*Othello* villain			
Superhero film for her, set in Africa (2 wds.)												
Really long time				___City (city-building video game)					Singer Bennett or actor Danza			

Answers on page 123

Football's Greatest

Scooby-Doo and Snoopy

People named after President Lincoln

Bruce Willis film series that's also a color

Classic sitcom set at the Sunshine Cab Company

Orange Thanksgiving vegetable

Kindergarten basics

The Scarlet ___

Football championship he's won 6 times (2 wds.)

___-ray disc

Jeff Probst line: "The ___ has spoken"

His first and last name

T-___ (*Jurassic Park* dino, for short)

"Your mission, should you choose to ___ it ..."

Gillette ___ (Foxborough field where he played)

Gang suffix, in *The Untouchables*

Village People hit sung with arm motions

University in Ann Arbor where he played

___ card (offstage help)

___ Star Pictures

Recede, as a tide

Einstein or Titan suffix, in element names

Wade's Supreme Court opponent

First or second part of a football game

Sound from Sneezy

Football down after the chains are moved

High cards in poker

___-portrait (many a van Gogh painting)

Like arguments made in court

Prefix with metric

Oldest of the Smurfs

Apocalypse Now setting, for short

Computer memory unit

Money left for a waitress

Tie-score breakers, for short

Angela Merkel or Heidi Klum's country

Marvel comic based on a Norse god

Pie ___ mode (2 wds.)

New England's football team

Pro football contest (inits. + wd.)

The ___ (2017 movie about a D.C. newspaper)

Answers on page 123

After 20 seasons with the New England Patriots, the star quarterback (here with his wife, model Gisele Bündchen) moved to the Tampa Bay Buccaneers in 2020.

T R I V I A !

1. Directed by John Krasinski, *A Quiet Place* stars the *Office* alum alongside his wife, Emily Blunt. Shortly after the horror film's release, *Saturday Night Live* parodied the movie, poking fun at which celebrity?

A. Kim Kardashian **B.** Kanye West
C. Meryl Streep   **D.** Justin Bieber

2. In a 2017 interview with *The New York Times, Get Out* director Jordan Peele discussed his inspirations. Which is the first movie that really scared him?

A. *Halloween*
B. *The Shining*
C. *A Nightmare on Elm Street*
D. *Night of the Living Dead*

3. In *Mamma Mia! Here We Go Again,* Lily James plays a younger version of Donna Sheridan. Before she played the dancing queen, she also brought to life which Disney princess?

A. Belle
B. Cinderella
C. Ariel
D. Aurora

4. The *Disaster Artist* actor and director James Franco first watched *The Room,* the Tommy Wiseau film that *Artist* is based around, while working on what movie?

A. *The Interview*
B. *This Is the End*
C. *Pineapple Express*
D. *Oz the Great and Powerful*

Movie Magic
How well do you know these buzzworthy blockbusters?

5. During her downtime, which *Girls Trip* costar did Tiffany Haddish take on a Groupon swamp tour?

A. Queen Latifah
B. Jada Pinkett-Smith
C. Regina Hall
D. Kate Walsh

6. Michael B. Jordan, who played Erik Killmonger in *Black Panther,* had already starred in a Marvel movie as what superhero?

A. The Human Torch
B. Nightcrawler
C. Mr. Fantastic
D. Spiderman

7. According to a 2018 interview with Collider, Steven Spielberg played what music on-set while filming *Ready Player One*?

A. The Bee Gees
B. The Beach Boys
C. ABBA
D. Elton John

8. *Ocean's 8,* the franchise installment featuring an all-female lead cast, is centered around a heist at what star-studded event?

A. The Oscars
B. The Emmys
C. The Met Gala
D. The SAG Awards

9. While working on Wes Anderson's *Isle of Dogs,* set in the futuristic Japanese city of Megasaki, roughly how many crew members were solely focusing on making the puppets, according to producer Jeremy Dawson?

A. 25   **B.** 60
C. 75   **D.** 30

10. What was the shortest movie Christopher Nolan has made since his 1998 feature debut, *Following*?

A. *Batman Begins* **B.** *Dunkirk*
C. *The Dark Knight* **D.** *Interstellar*

ANSWERS Movies: 1B. 2C. 3B. 4A. 5B. 6A. 7A. 8C. 9B. 10B. Johnson; 1B. 2C. Gadot; 1B. 2C. 3C. 4B. 5D.

Rock and Roll
Dwayne Johnson

1. In college Johnson seriously considered a different career path, until a professor explained just how much more schooling he would need. What did Johnson want to do?

A. A surgeon
B. An FBI or CIA agent
C. An accountant
D. A prosecutor

2. "It's here in _____ that I had a hard time staying on the right track and had a hard time staying in school and had a lot of arrests doing things I shouldn't be doing," Johnson told *Variety*, reflecting on his teenage years. What state was Johnson referring to?

A. New York   **B.** California
C. Hawaii   **D.** North Dakota

The Great Gal
Wonder Woman's Powerful Lead

1. Where did Gal Gadot meet her husband, real estate developer Yaron Varsano?

A. On a safari
B. In the desert
C. On the red carpet
D. At a nightclub

2. Gadot auditioned for the role of a Bond girl in 2008's *Quantum of Solace*, but it went to another actress. Who got the role instead?

A. Eva Green
B. Caterina Murino
C. Olga Kurylenko
D. Rosamund Pike

3. What did Gadot tell *Glamour* in 2017 that she could watch on television for hours?

A. *The Bachelor*
B. *Game of Thrones*
C. Cooking shows
D. *The Real Housewives*

4. What song did Gadot play in her trailer to psych herself up for her *Batman v Superman* audition?

A. "Born This Way" by Lady Gaga
B. "Run the World" by Beyoncé
C. "Girl on Fire" by Alicia Keys
D. "Fighter" by Christina Aguilera

5. Billionaire Roman Abramovich bought Gal and her husband's luxury hotel the Varsano in 2015. Who is Abramovich's reported celeb BFF?

A. Denzel Washington
B. Jennifer Lopez
C George Clooney
D. Leonardo DiCaprio

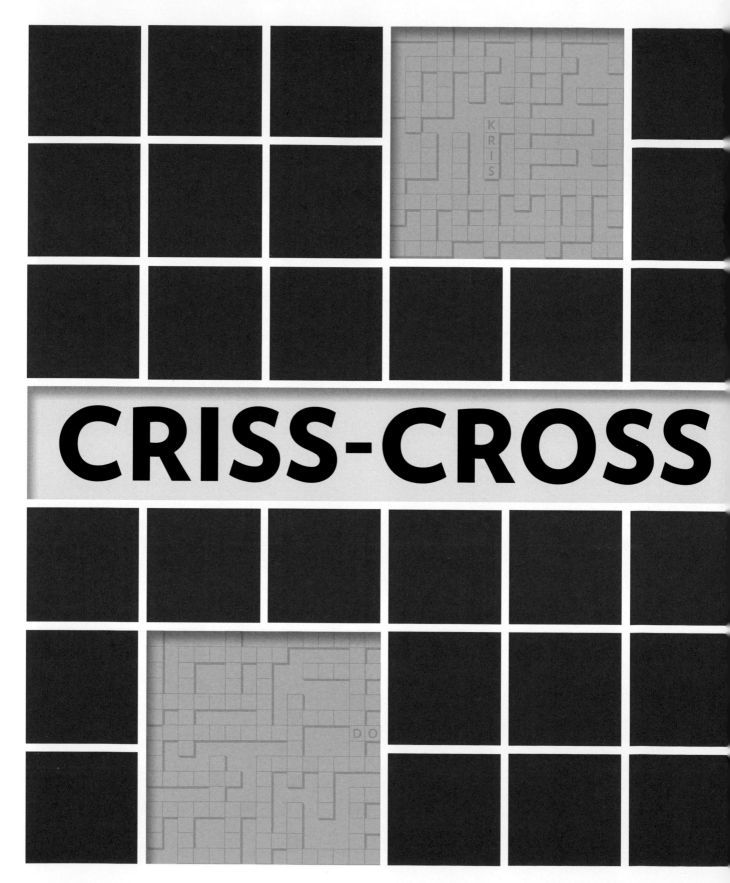

CRISS-CROSS

For criss-cross puzzles, place the words from the list into the grid. There's only one way they'll all fit, and we've given you a starter clue. When you're done, unscramble the letters in the tinted squares to answer a bonus question. Viola Davis, Ellen DeGeneres, Justin Bieber and Anthony Hopkins are counting on you.

Talk Show Host

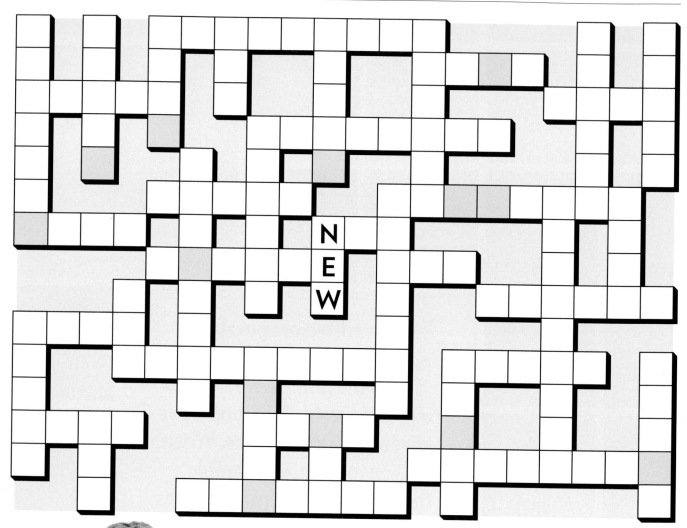

3 letters	**4 letters**	SHOW	JUDGE	SITCOM
CBS	DORY	**5 letters**	PIXAR	TREVOR
GIG	EDTV	ELLEN	TEXAS	**7 letters**
MET	EMMY	EPCOT	VEGAN	ACTRESS
NBC	FROG	GAMES	**6 letters**	DE ROSSI
~~NEW~~	IDOL	GIANT	CHEESE	EXPRESS
QVC	MUCH	HUMOR	PENNEY	**8 letters**
TOP	NEMO	JOKES	PORTIA	AMERICAN

HEADLINE
PRODUCER
RICHMOND
9 letters
CONEHEADS
COVERGIRL
DEGENERES

Read the shaded letters (from left to right and top to bottom) to reveal a job Ellen DeGeneres had before making it as a stand-up comic:

Answers on page **124**

Pop Star Prince

BIEBER

3 letters	4 letters	5 letters	6 letters	7 letters	9 letters
AMA	BABY	ACTOR	BAD DAY	ONE TIME	DESPACITO
BIG	BEAT	CLEAR	~~BIEBER~~	ONTARIO	GUATEMALA
FAN	DREW	EENIE	CANADA	PURPOSE	MISTLETOE
NOW	LIVE	LOLLY	FRENCH	YOUTUBE	**10 letters**
POP	PRAY	NEVER	GRAMMY	**8 letters**	GIRLFRIEND
R&B	RBMG	SPREE	SELENA	RECOVERY	SONGWRITER
SAY	TEEN	UNDER	SINGER		

Read the shaded letters (from left to right and top to bottom) to reveal what pop star's former L.A. home Justin Bieber also once lived in:

Answers on page **124**

Reality TV Star

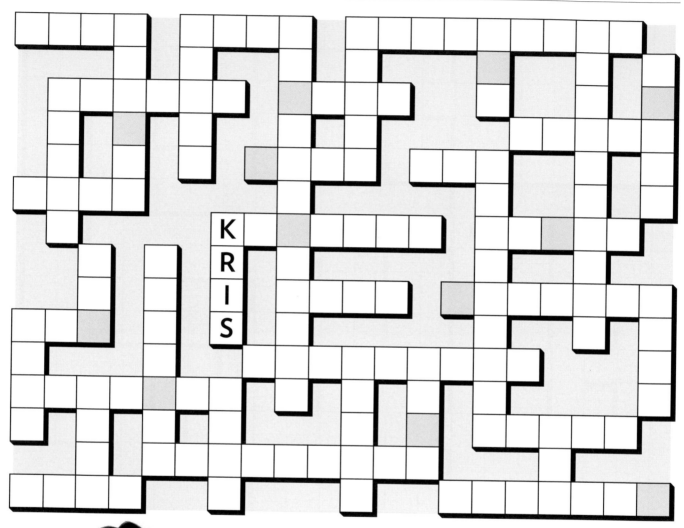

3 letters	DASH	RICH	KANYE	**7 letters**	HYPNOTIZE
CSI	EARN	TAPE	MIAMI	DANCING	INSTAGRAM
DVD	ELLE	TRUE	MODEL	KEEPING	RASPBERRY
JAM	GOLD	YOGA	PARIS	KENDALL	**10 letters**
KIM	KISS	**5 letters**	STARS	SELFISH	CALIFORNIA
ROB	KRIS	ALIEN	**6 letters**	STYLIST	**12 letters**
4 letters	MARK	BREAK	BALLAS	**9 letters**	KONFIDENTIAL
AWAY	NOEL	FLESH	HILTON	FRAGRANCE	

Read the shaded letters (from left to right and top to bottom) to reveal the *only* place Kim Kardashian says she will wear flat shoes:

Answers on page **124**

The reality star (left, with sisters Khloé and Kylie in 2019) and family announced that the 20th season of their E! network series would be their last.

Westworld Genius

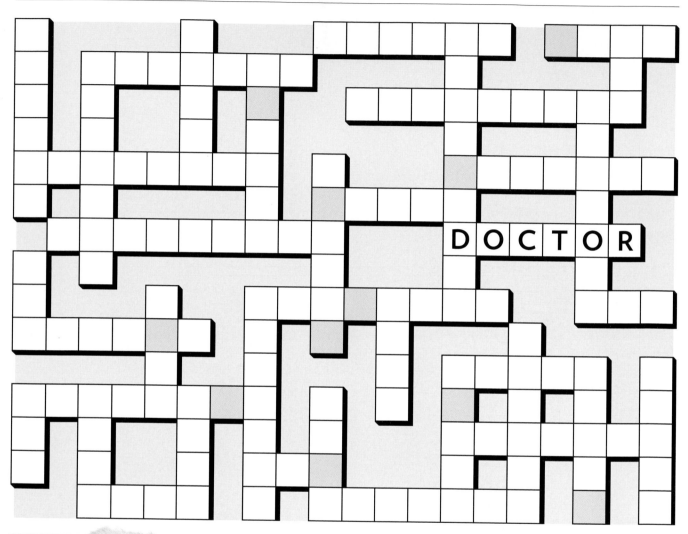

DOCTOR

3 letters	EDGE	CROSS	GRINCH	CHARING	INSTINCT
EVE	EMMA	MAGIC	INDIAN	DEMILLE	**9 letters**
MAN	FORD	NIXON	LECTER	DRACULA	COMMANDER
RED	NOAH	OCEAN	PHILIP	DRESSER	GLAMORGAN
SIR	SOME	SPICY	SOLACE	FASTEST	WESTWORLD
YES	THOR	**6 letters**	**7 letters**	**8 letters**	
4 letters	**5 letters**	~~DOCTOR~~	AMISTAD	ELEPHANT	
AURA	CECIL	DRAGON	ANTHONY	FRACTURE	

Read the shaded letters (from left to right and top to bottom) to reveal the first actor to read for Anthony Hopkins's eventual role in *Silence of the Lambs*:

Answers on
page **124**

Thursday Night Favorite

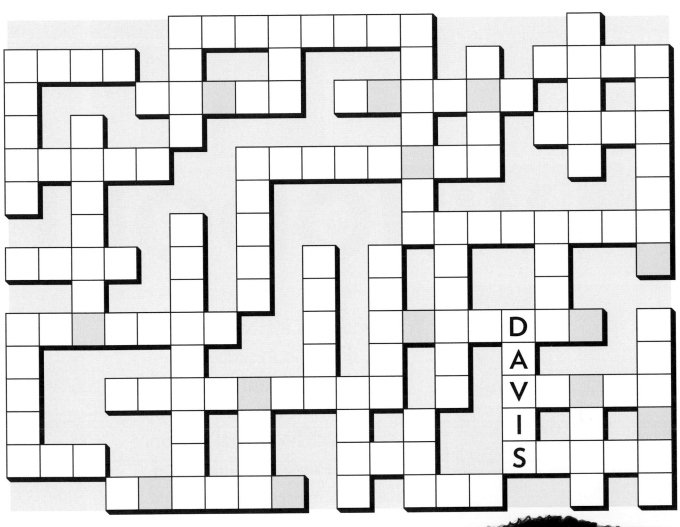

3 letters
AGE
AMY
EAT
OUT
SAG

4 letters
HACK

LILA
MAID
OBIE
OPUS
ROSE
RUBY
TARA
TONY

TRIO

5 letters
CLARK
DAVIS
DOUBT
JUVEE
NAVAL
OASIS

RHODE
SIGHT
SQUAD
TONYA
VIOLA

6 letters
AMANDA
HEDLEY

ISLAND
TENNON

7 letters
KEATING
MINERVA
SCANDAL
SUICIDE
THE HELP

8 letters
AIBILEEN
CORDUROY
MCCOLLUM

9 letters
JUILLIARD
PRISONERS

Read the shaded letters (from left to right and top to bottom) to reveal the actor whose Italian villa Viola Davis stayed at on her honeymoon:

Answers on page **124**

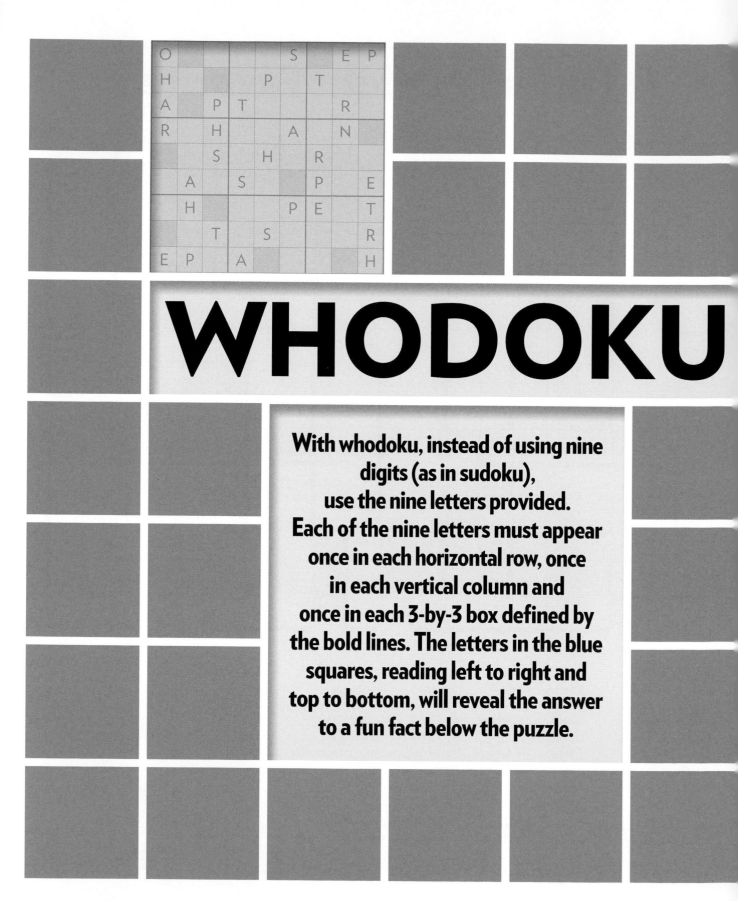

WHODOKU

With whodoku, instead of using nine
digits (as in sudoku),
use the nine letters provided.
Each of the nine letters must appear
once in each horizontal row, once
in each vertical column and
once in each 3-by-3 box defined by
the bold lines. The letters in the blue
squares, reading left to right and
top to bottom, will reveal the answer
to a fun fact below the puzzle.

With acrostics, as you answer the clues, transfer the letters to the same-numbered squares in the grid. The letters in the grid, reading left to right and top to bottom, will spell out a trivia fact related to the celeb. Work back and forth between the grid and clues to solve the puzzle. Don't worry, Ryan Reynolds, Amy Poehler and Hugh Jackman have your back!

ACROSTIC

1-K	2-B	3-H	4-D	5-G
16-E	17-G	18-C	19-A	20-H
	32-I	33-C	34-H	
45-E	46-A	47-I	48-C	49-H
	59-D	60-J	61-F	62-K

Master of Music

USE THESE NINE LETTERS

S
H
A
R
P
N
O
T
E

Answers on page 125

O					S		E	P
H				P		T		
A		P	T				R	
R		H			A		N	
		S		H		R		
	A		S			P		E
	H				P	E		T
		T		S				R
E	P		A					H

THE LETTERS IN THE BLUE SQUARES, READING TOP TO BOTTOM AND LEFT TO RIGHT, REVEAL A FUN FACT.
In 2007 Lin-Manuel Miranda played a bellhop pushing a luggage cart on what TV show?

Ace Actress

USE THESE
NINE
LETTERS

S
T
O
N
E
G
R
A
D

Answers on
page 125

A	S							G
			A	G	S		D	
T		O		R				N
O			S		G	R		E
	E						G	
D		G	R		N			A
R				T		G		O
	A		O	N	R			
E							A	R

THE LETTERS IN THE BLUE SQUARES, READING TOP TO BOTTOM AND LEFT TO RIGHT, REVEAL A FUN FACT.
Emma Stone's first job was working in a bakery baking what?

Venom Star

USE THESE NINE LETTERS

G O L D M I N E R

Answers on page 125

D		N		G				L
	E		L			G		
L	G	I			N			E
	L			N		I		
N			D		O			G
			M	E			N	
G			E			N	O	D
		E			G		L	
O				R		E		M

THE LETTERS IN THE BLUE SQUARES, READING TOP TO BOTTOM AND LEFT TO RIGHT, REVEAL A FUN FACT.
In 1998, making his TV debut, Tom Hardy won what kind of contest on a British morning show?

Movie Ringmaster

1-C	2-I		3-G	4-K	5-F	6-G	7-A	8-I	9-J	10-E	11-B	12-H	13-D		14-G	15-B	16-J
17-F	18-E	19-J		20-J	21-K	22-A	23-E	24-C	25-D	26-I	27-B	28-G		29-A	30-E	31-C	32-G
33-H	34-E		35-C	36-G	37-A	38-D	39-E	40-J	41-I		42-I	43-F	44-E	45-K	46-D	47-A	
48-J	49-G	50-A	51-B	52-I	53-D	54-E	55-C		56-A	57-C	58-D	59-G		60-H	61-E	62-D	63-K
64-J	65-K	66-I		67-E	68-A	69-B	70-D		71-A	72-C	73-B	74-F	75-G	76-I			

A. Country where Hugh was born: ___ ___ ___ ___ ___ ___ ___ ___ ___
                                          7 37 47 56 29 71 22 50 68

B. Yellow, pill-shaped henchman in *Despicable Me*: ___ ___ ___ ___ ___ ___
                                                     69 73 51 11 15 27

C. *Van* ___ (2004 film starring Hugh as a monster hunter):

___ ___ ___ ___ ___ ___ ___
57 24 31 35 1 72 55

D. Rudolph, Comet or Blitzen: ___ ___ ___ ___ ___ ___ ___ ___
                            62 70 53 13 38 46 58 25

E. Medium on which Hugh hosted the Oscars and the Tonys:

___ ___ ___ ___ ___ ___ ___ ___ ___ ___
10 61 44 34 23 18 67 39 30 54

F. ___ *Alone* (Kevin vs. the "Wet Bandits" movie): ___ ___ ___ ___
                                                       17 43 74 5

G. Movie about a dancing penguin named Mumble (Hugh voiced Memphis):

___ ___ ___ ___ ___   ___ ___ ___ ___
49 75 3 6 59   14 28 32 36

H. *Horton Hears a . . .* ___ ___ ___
                            60 33 12

I. Like hands or feet after they've been in the water a long time:

___ ___ ___ ___ ___ ___ ___ ___
42 8 26 2 52 76 66 41

J. Patrick who plays Professor X in *X-Men:* ___ ___ ___ ___ ___ ___ ___
                                                19 64 40 20 9 16 48

K. Float just above the ground, like a flying saucer: ___ ___ ___ ___ ___
                                                     65 21 45 63 4

Answers on page 125

Hugh Jackman

Deadpool Dad

1-C	2-B	3-G	4-H	5-D '	6-E		7-J		8-E	9-A	10-K	11-I	12-G	13-K	14-C	15-F	16-G
	17-F	18-G		19-I	20-H	21-G	22-A		23-C	24-B	25-H	26-G	27-E	28-E	29-I	30-F '	
31-C	32-A	33-B	34-K	35-H	36-G	37-E	38-J		39-B	40-F	41-E	42-G	43-D	44-A	45-G		46-I
47-F	48-H	49-A	50-K	51-E	52-C	53-E	54-G		55-F	56-K	57-A	58-H		59-K	60-D	61-I	62-G
	63-K	64-A	65-F	66-G	67-J	68-B		69-J	70-K	71-H		72-D	73-B	74-A	75-I	

Ryan Reynolds

A. Like Ryan Reynolds (from British Columbia) or Alex Trebek (from Ontario):

‾‾ ‾‾ ‾‾ ‾‾ ‾‾ ‾‾ ‾‾ ‾‾
64　9　44　49　74　57　32　22

B. Trio granted by a genie: ‾‾ ‾‾ ‾‾ ‾‾ ‾‾ ‾‾
39　73　33　2　24　68

C. Animated film about a racing snail, voiced by Ryan: ‾‾ ‾‾ ‾‾ ‾‾ ‾‾
1　14　23　31　52

D. Snap, as a football from the center to the quarterback: ‾‾ ‾‾ ‾‾ ‾‾
60　43　72　5

E. *National ___ Van Wilder* (film for Ryan): ‾‾ ‾‾ ‾‾ ‾‾ ‾‾ ‾‾ ‾‾ , ‾‾
28　41　8　51　27　53　37　6

F. Flowers that are "pushed up" in a graveyard: ‾‾ ‾‾ ‾‾ ‾‾ ‾‾ ‾‾ ‾‾
47　65　15　30　17　40　55

G. "Colorful" DC superhero (with a glowing ring) played by Ryan in 2011:

‾‾ ‾‾ ‾‾ ‾‾ ‾‾　‾‾ ‾‾ ‾‾ ‾‾ ‾‾ ‾‾ ‾‾
45　42　3　12　18　54　21　16　62　36　66　26

H. Film genre involving a sleuth: ‾‾ ‾‾ ‾‾ ‾‾ ‾‾ ‾‾ ‾‾
35　25　71　58　48　4　20

I. Bullock in *The Proposal* with Ryan: ‾‾ ‾‾ ‾‾ ‾‾ ‾‾ ‾‾
75　46　11　29　19　61

J. Furnace output: ‾‾ ‾‾ ‾‾ ‾‾
69　67　7　38

K. Narrowed one's eyes, as Clint Eastwood is famous for doing:

‾‾ ‾‾ ‾‾ ‾‾ ‾‾ ‾‾ ‾‾ ‾‾
63　13　56　70　10　59　34　50

Answers on page 125

Queen of Laughs

1-K	2-B	3-H	4-D	5-G		6-H	7-B	8-D	9-C	10-F	11-A	12-G	13-J		14-F	15-C	
16-E	17-G	18-C	19-A	20-H	21-B		22-A	23-B	24-J	25-E	26-F	27-D	28-A ,		29-A	30-G	31-C
	32-I	33-C	34-H		35-F	36-H		37-K	38-A		39-J	40-H	41-B	42-A	43-E	44-G	
45-E	46-A	47-I	48-C	49-H		50-K	51-F	52-A	53-J	54-I		55-J	56-E		57-B	58-D	
	59-D	60-J	61-F	62-K	63-A	64-C ,	65-H		66-F	67-D	68-E	69-B	70-J	71-C	72-I		

A. *Parks and* ___ (sitcom Amy starred in for seven seasons):

__ __ __ __ __ __ __ __ __ __
42 28 22 46 63 29 19 11 52 38

B. *Star Wars: Episode I—The* ___ *Menace:* __ __ __ __ __ __ __
41 2 69 21 7 23 57

C. ___ *Night Live* (Amy won a 2016 Emmy for hosting it):

__ __ __ __ __ __ __ __
18 71 15 48 64 9 33 31

D. In a gloomy, dejected way: __ __ __ __ __ __
27 67 8 59 4 58

E. *The Golden* ___ (award show Amy cohosted 2013-15):

__ __ __ __ __ __
45 25 43 16 68 56

F. *30 Rock* star who co-anchored "Weekend Update" with Amy:

__ __ __ __ __ __ __
61 35 51 14 66 26 10

G. Snake poison: __ __ __ __ __
44 5 12 17 30

H. *The* ___ (show in which Amy voiced Bart's future girlfriend and ex-wife):

__ __ __ __ __ __ __ __
6 3 40 49 34 20 36 65

I. Red carpet dress: __ __ __ __
72 47 32 54

J. *Deuce* ___ *: Male Gigolo* (Amy played Ruth): __ __ __ __ __ __ __
70 39 13 55 24 60 53

K. *Black* ___ *Down* (named for a bird): __ __ __ __
62 37 1 50

Answers on page **125**

Amy Poehler

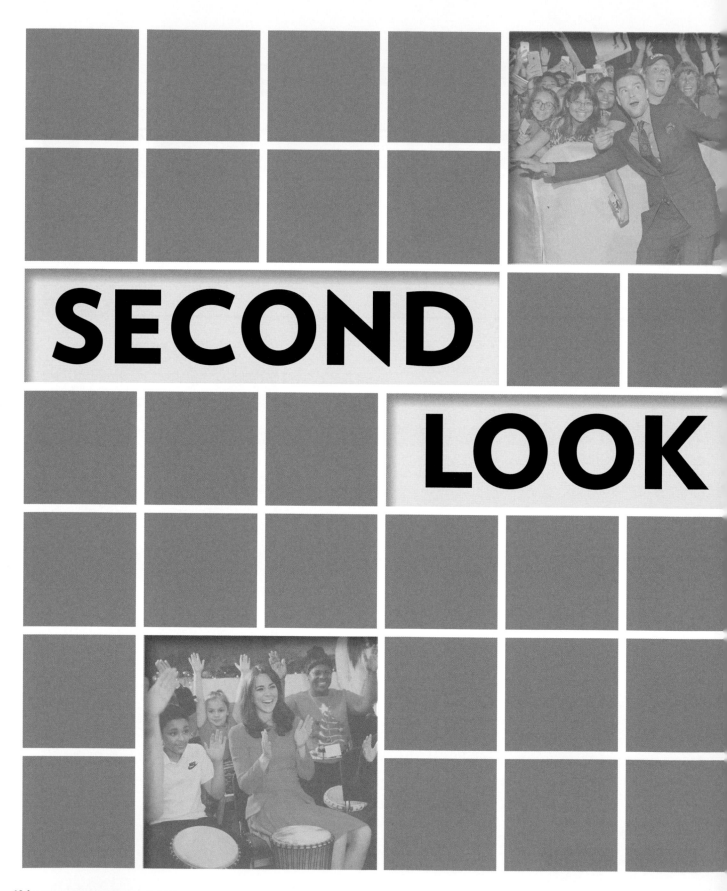

SECOND LOOK

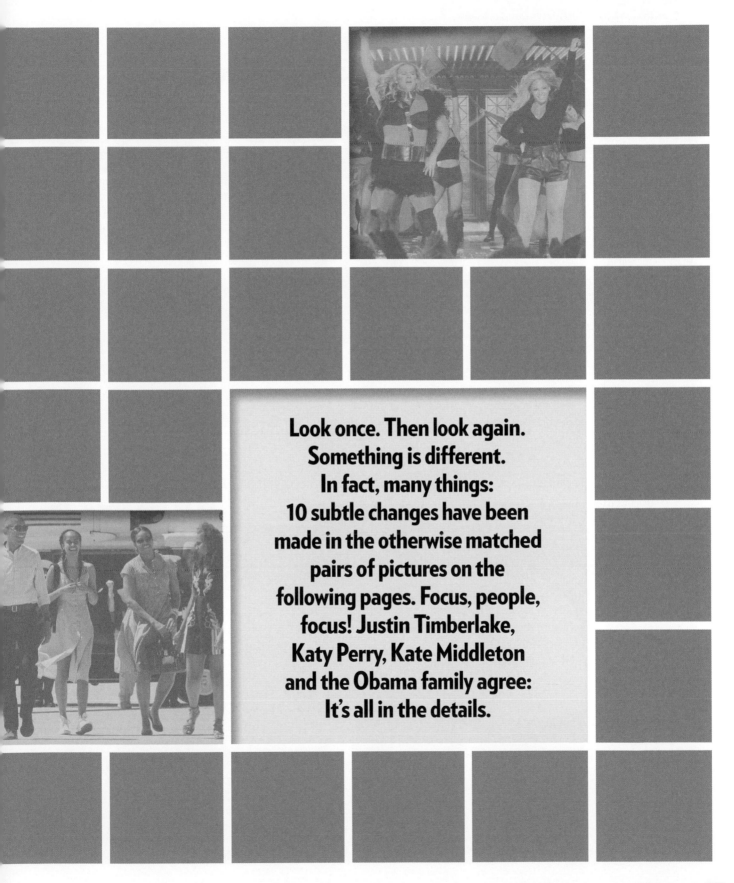

Look once. Then look again.
Something is different.
In fact, many things:
10 subtle changes have been
made in the otherwise matched
pairs of pictures on the
following pages. Focus, people,
focus! Justin Timberlake,
Katy Perry, Kate Middleton
and the Obama family agree:
It's all in the details.

Royal Role Model

Prince Harry showed off his skills at London's Lord's Cricket Ground to celebrate the club's Coach Core apprenticeship program on Oct. 7, 2016. The prince met with supporters of the program, designed by Harry and his brother and sister-in-law the Duke and Duchess of Cambridge, which works with young adults in disadvantaged communities to be leaders, coaches and role models.

10
CHANGES
KEEP SCORE

Answers on page 126

Seeing Double

Channing Tatum received a helping hand from Beyoncé while performing "Run the World (Girls)" on *Lip Sync Battle* in Los Angeles. Tatum, who was competing against then-wife Jenna Dewan Tatum's striptease performance set to Ginuwine's "Pony," took the stage in full Queen B style and surprised everyone with a cameo from the superstar herself. "What. Just. Happened," a shocked Dewan Tatum tweeted.

10
**CHANGES
KEEP SCORE**

☐ ☐
☐ ☐
☐ ☐
☐ ☐
☐ ☐

Answers on page 126

Healthy Hangout

Chef **Bobby Flay**, actor **Adrian Grenier**, chef **Tom Colicchio** and rapper-actor **Common** joined forces for an unlikely lunch date at the launch of Naked Juice's #DrinkGood DoGood campaign in New York City on Aug. 3, 2016. The charitable initiative's goal is to erase America's food deserts, areas in which it is difficult to buy fresh food, and to donate fresh produce to people in need.

10
CHANGES
KEEP SCORE

Answers on page 126

Crowd-Pleaser

Justin Timberlake posed for photos with fans at the premiere of the Netflix special *Justin Timberlake + the Tennessee Kids* at the Toronto International Film Festival on Sept. 13, 2016. The documentary follows the pop star's last performance of his two-year-long world tour the 20/20 Experience, which featured 134 shows and is billed as one of the highest-grossing of the decade.

10 CHANGES
KEEP SCORE

☐ ☐
☐ ☐
☐ ☐
☐ ☐
☐ ☐

Answers on page **126**

A Very Popular Guy

Pope Francis met with the public at the Vatican on Dec. 21, 2016. Francis holds weekly general-audience visits whenever he is in Rome, giving pilgrims and visitors a chance to see him in person. During the meetings, Francis leads prayers and small teachings in more than six languages, including English, before imparting his apostolic blessing upon the crowd.

10
CHANGES
KEEP SCORE

Answers on page 126

Teenage Dream

The students of Loreto Mandeville Hall Toorak in Melbourne got the chance of a lifetime when **Katy Perry** (channeling Frida Kahlo) stopped by the all-girls Catholic school Nov. 13, 2014, to dole out some advice. Most important of all? "Don't let boys distract you," Perry said, adding that there's nothing more empowering than knowledge. "Fantastic 1st day in Melb," the singer later tweeted.

10
**CHANGES
KEEP SCORE**

☐ ☐
☐ ☐
☐ ☐
☐ ☐
☐ ☐

Answers on page **126**

Rebel in Red

Madonna worked the stage during her Rebel Heart tour stop in Taipei, Taiwan, on Feb. 4, 2016. The pop star treated the crowd to a rare performance of her 1994 hit "Take a Bow." Despite the song's being a No. 1 smash for the superstar, she had never before included it in her concert set lists and had only performed it live a few times, most recently at the 1995 American Music Awards.

10
CHANGES
KEEP SCORE

Answers on page 126

Peace in the Kingdom

Former *Good Morning America* host **Michael Strahan** flashes the peace sign while hanging with comedian **Chris Rock** and **Chip** and **Dale** at Disney's Animal Kingdom in Bay Lake, Fla., on Aug. 18, 2015. The former New York Giants defensive end and his *Madagascar: Escape 2 Africa* star pal took a break from their sunny vacation with family and friends to goof off with the adventure-loving chipmunks.

10
CHANGES
KEEP SCORE

Answers on page 126

Christmas Cuties

Very merry Mouseketeers! **Mariah Carey** is joined by her then 5-year-old twins **Moroccan** and **Monroe Cannon** onstage during a concert at Disneyland in Anaheim, Calif., on Nov. 16, 2016. The "All I Want for Christmas Is You" singer had recently split from fiancé James Packer ahead of the debut of her reality series *Mariah's World,* which ran for one season.

10
CHANGES
KEEP
SCORE

Answers on page 126

Jumping Jones

Comedian **Leslie Jones** leaped for joy in the final minutes of a New York Knicks game against the Philadelphia 76ers at Madison Square Garden on April 12, 2017. The former *Saturday Night Live* star sat courtside at the game, which was the final one of the regular season and ended with the Knicks winning by one point after an action-packed fourth quarter.

10 CHANGES KEEP SCORE

Answers on page 126

America's First Dad

President Barack Obama heads back to the White House with **Malia, Michelle** and **Sasha** after a weekend trip to Yosemite National Park on June 19, 2016. The then-First Family celebrated their last Father's Day in office at the park and also marked the 100-year anniversary of the National Park Service. "Happy Father's Day to all the dads out there," he tweeted.

10
CHANGES
KEEP SCORE

Answers on page 126

Drumming Duchess

Kate Middleton celebrates the holidays at the Anna Freud Centre Family School, a leading research charity. Showing off her drumming skills, the Duchess of Cambridge played a rendition of Queen's "We Will Rock You" with the students on Dec. 15, 2015, in London. The school's Christmas party celebrated improvements the children have made in their communication skills.

10
CHANGES
KEEP SCORE

☐ ☐
☐ ☐
☐ ☐
☐ ☐
☐ ☐

Answers on page 126

ANSWERS

How'd you do? Check yourself and calculate your bragging rights—or get a little help. (We said a *little!*)

CROSSWORDS

Page 8: Zoë Saldana

```
SAM   COP   ALAN
OWEN  AVA   RISE
NENE  RAY   EVIL
   ECO   ONEAL
ZOESALDANA
AARON  OLE   END
CHIN   INS  ALIE
SUN   RAN   CRANE
   LENADUNHAM
ALOAD      ABE
BABY   LIV  TOED
ATIE   ELI  TREE
DEER   ELS   ARE
```

Page 9: Ed Sheeran

```
MAKE   AMP   OBI
ONIT  LEGO   RAT
EDSHEERAN   CBS
SAT  DRE  STAY
   SIT  BEE
SHAPE  OUTLOUD
RIPA  RED  LUNA
SPECTOR  TERMS
   EAT  GER
  HAYS  SAM  BIG
GIL  KATYPERRY
OLE  SAUL  TEAM
TLC  ABE  CASS
```

Page 10: Jennifer Lawrence

```
SEAS  AJAR  EPA
OAHU  LOBO  SEE
BRADLEYCOOPER
  DYE    TONTO
  BAER  DASH
JENNIFER  STAN
EEN  COCOA  AMY
DRAG  LAWRENCE
  RUDY  RUSS
ATLAS   IOR
LIAMHEMSWORTH
END  EVEN  PAIR
CAD  RELO  EYES
```

Page 11: Serena Williams

```
MAC    LEE    MAN
AGA   DONT  PIKE
SER   ALDA  ARIE
SERENA    STAND
  ODE   PAT
HOLD   WILLIAMS
OWL  VENUS  TAI
WESTERNS   ALEX
   EIE   ORA
SEVEN    AGENTS
OPEN  MEIR  TIL
OPRY  HIDE  INA
NSA   ONA   SAM
```

Page 12: Emma Watson

```
GAME  ROB   HIS
ETAT  ONE  DARK
NOAH  SIA  AWAY
EMMAWATSON
  NOR  TRIAL
AWL  KID  KENYA
LIAR  ODS  LOOK
STRUT  SAO  DNA
 HANOI  NIC
  WALLFLOWER
EZRA  LEO  LADI
DORY  BAR  OWEN
SOS   END  RANG
```

Page 13: Will Smith

```
JETT  RAH   BAD
ALAI  ELIS  ALA
WILLSMITH   LIL
SEETO   COLLIE
  SON  HOO
IAM  NOW  SLEEP
ALEC  MEN  LETO
NELLS  EAR  RAP
  EAT  SAM
THEORY   LEONI
REA  ANNAFARIS
ODD  HARI  RENO
TYS  NAR  ALAN
```

Page 14: Kate McKinnon

```
MOWS  ADM  FLAV
OLIN  MAE  ROMA
NYLE  URL  AGIN
KATEMCKINNON
  ZAK  SAC
BADER  OSMONDS
BIO   TWA   POL
CLINTON  PARTY
  IAN  TEM
 JUSTINBIEBER
DOCS  GOO  LENO
ISLA  HSN  IRIS
STAN  TEE  AIDY
```

Page 16: Chris Pratt

```
ENYA  MATT  LAW
RAES  AMOR  ALE
ISAT  NOTI  NON
CHRIS      PRATT
  NAS  ASI
EON   MEAN  LIZA
SNOW  VIN  ELON
SEDA  EDER  LET
  LEN  SIA
WORLD    PARKS
ABE  DERN  REAL
RIB  ILIE  ONTO
SEA  EMME  NEST
```

PAGE 16

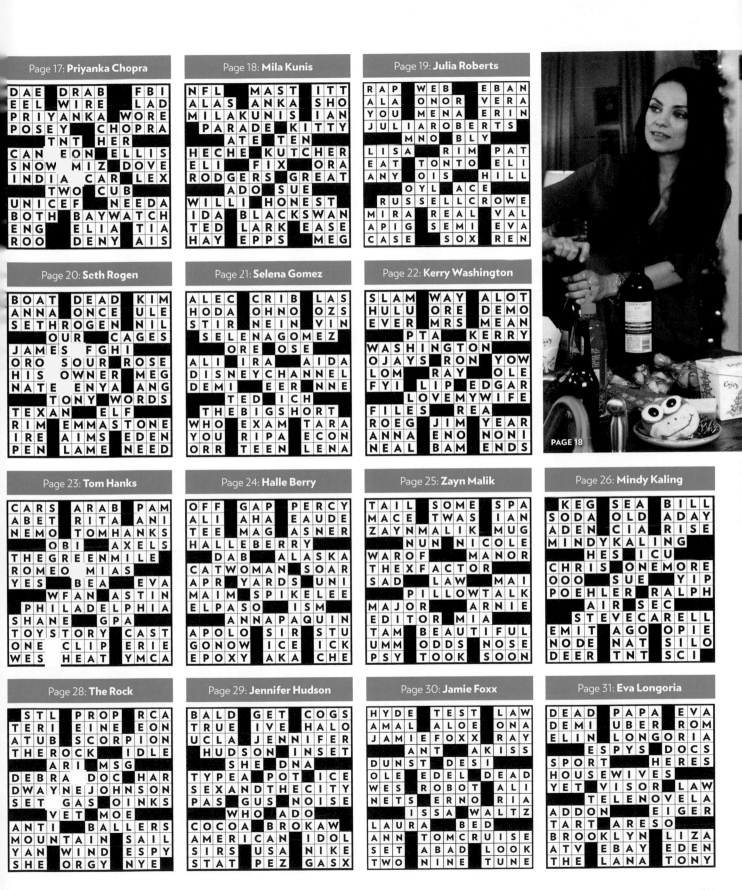

Page 17: Priyanka Chopra

```
DAE  DRAB     FBI
EEL  WIRE     LAD
PRIYANKA  WORE
POSEY    CHOPRA
     TNT  HER
CAN  EON  ELLIS
SNOW MIZ  DOVE
INDIA CAR LEX
TWO  CUB
UNICEF   NEEDA
BOTH  BAYWATCH
ENG   ELIA  TIA
ROO   DENY  AIS
```

Page 18: Mila Kunis

```
NFL  MAST  ITT
ALAS ANKA  SHO
MILAKUNIS  IAN
PARADE    KITTY
ATE  TEN
HECHE   KUTCHER
ELI  FIX   ORA
RODGERS   GREAT
ADO   SUE
WILLI   HONEST
IDA  BLACKSWAN
TED  LARK  EASE
HAY  EPPS  MEG
```

Page 19: Julia Roberts

```
RAP  WEB    EBAN
ALA  ONOR   VERA
YOU  MENA   ERIN
JULIAROBERTS
MNO    BLY
LISA  RIM   PAT
EAT  TONTO  ELI
ANY  OIS    HILL
OYL  ACE
RUSSELLCROWE
MIRA  REAL  VAL
APIG  SEMI  EVA
CASE  SOX   REN
```

Page 20: Seth Rogen

```
BOAT DEAD  KIM
ANNA ONCE  ULE
SETHROGEN  NIL
OUR    CAGES
JAMES  FGHI
ORO SOUR  ROSE
HIS OWNER MEG
NATE ENYA ANG
TONY  WORDS
TEXAN  ELF
RIM  EMMASTONE
IRE  AIMS  EDEN
PEN  LAME  NEED
```

Page 21: Selena Gomez

```
ALEC CRIB  LAS
HODA OHNO  OZS
STIR NEIN  VIN
SELENAGOMEZ
ORE    OSE
ALI  IRA   AIDA
DISNEYCHANNEL
DEMI   EER  NNE
TED    ICH
THEBIGSHORT
WHO EXAM  TARA
YOU RIPA  ECON
ORR TEEN  LENA
```

Page 22: Kerry Washington

```
SLAM WAY  ALOT
HULU ORE  DEMO
EVER MRS  MEAN
PTA    KERRY
WASHINGTON
OJAYS RON  YOW
LOM  RAY   OLE
FYI  LIP   EDGAR
LOVEMYWIFE
FILES    REA
ROEG  JIM  YEAR
ANNA  ENO  NONI
NEAL  BAM  ENDS
```

Page 23: Tom Hanks

```
CARS ARAB  PAM
ABET RITA  ANI
NEMO  TOMHANKS
OBI    AXELS
THEGREENMILE
ROMEO  MIAS
YES  BEA    EVA
WFAN   ASTIN
PHILADELPHIA
SHANE    GPA
TOYSTORY  CAST
ONE  CLIP  ERIE
WES  HEAT  YMCA
```

Page 24: Halle Berry

```
OFF  GAP  PERCY
ALI  AHA  EAUDE
TEE  MAG  ASNER
HALLEBERRY
DAB    ALASKA
CATWOMAN  SOAR
APR  YARDS UNI
MAIM  SPIKELEE
ELPASO   ISM
ANNAPAQUIN
APOLO SIR  STU
GONOW ICE  ICK
EPOXY AKA  CHE
```

Page 25: Zayn Malik

```
TAIL SOME  SPA
MACE TWAS  IAN
ZAYNMALIK  MUG
NUN   NICOLE
WAROF   MANOR
THEXFACTOR
SAD    LAW   MAI
PILLOWTALK
MAJOR   ARNIE
EDITOR  MIA
TAM  BEAUTIFUL
UMM  ODDS  NOSE
PSY  TOOK  SOON
```

Page 26: Mindy Kaling

```
KEG  SEA   BILL
SODA OLD   ADAY
ADEN CIA   RISE
MINDYKALING
HES    ICU
CHRIS   ONEMORE
OOO   SUE   YIP
POEHLER   RALPH
AIR    SEC
STEVECARELL
EMIT  AGO   OPIE
NODE  NAT   SILO
DEER  TNT   SCI
```

Page 28: The Rock

```
STL  PROP  RCA
TERI EINE  EON
ATUB  SCORPION
THEROCK   IDLE
ARI   MSG
DEBRA DOC  HAR
DWAYNEJOHNSON
SET  GAS   OINKS
VET   MOE
ANTI   BALLERS
MOUNTAIN   SAIL
YAN  WIND  ESPY
SHE  ORGY  NYE
```

Page 29: Jennifer Hudson

```
BALD GET   COGS
TRUE IVE   HALO
UCLA  JENNIFER
HUDSON    INSET
SHE   DNA
TYPEA POT  ICE
SEXANDTHECITY
PAS  GUS   NOISE
WHO   ADO
COCOA   BROKAW
AMERICAN   IDOL
SIRS  USA  NIKE
STAT  PEZ  GASX
```

Page 30: Jamie Foxx

```
HYDE TEST  LAW
AMAL ALOE  ONA
JAMIEFOXX  RAY
ANT    AKISS
DUNST   DESI
OLE  EDEL  DEAD
WES  ROBOT ALI
NETS ERNO  RIA
ISSA   WALTZ
LAURA   BED
ANN  TOMCRUISE
SET  ABAD  LOOK
TWO  NINE  TUNE
```

Page 31: Eva Longoria

```
DEAD PAPA  EVA
DEMI UBER  ROM
ELIN  LONGORIA
ESPYS    DOCS
SPORT    HERES
HOUSEWIVES
YET  VISOR LAW
TELENOVELA
ADDON    EIGER
TART   ARESO
BROOKLYN  LIZA
ATV  EBAY  EDEN
THE  LANA  TONY
```

PAGE 18

CROSSWORDS (continued)

Page 32: Jake Gyllenhaal

```
ALPS  UMA   NERD
BEAK  RON   AREA
COLUMBIA    TINY
    LOA  JAKE
GYLLENHAAL
RUE      AFRICAN
AMFM  SGT  EURO
NATASHA    JIM
  SOURCECODE
  CITY   ATO
RACE  SLICKERS
OVER  KEN  IDEA
BETS  YEE  ESPN
```

Page 33: Sofia Vergara

```
ABC   RASP  DKNY
LEA   ISLE  IYAM
PER   BEAN  ERIC
SOFIAVERGARA
LAS        LOO
UNIVISION    LAG
FUN   COP   EGO
ONE   TRUEBLOOD
   BEA     IAN
DAVIDBECKHAM
EVIL  BRIE  RAY
LOEB  LIAR  DRE
INSO  ENOS  OKS
```

Page 34: Kevin Hart

```
ACME  LEAP  VAT
REAL  OPIE  IWO
KEVINHART   RAN
    NIA   SCARY
LAD   CNBC  OLDS
ONRIO      YEAR
LITTLEFOCKERS
    SELA  TYSON
SHAM  KRIS  POL
TYLER      RUE
REO   SNOOPDOGG
ANN   VEIN  EDIE
WAG   PODS  NEST
```

Page 35: Cher

```
CHER  MTS   HAIL
HODA  AHA   ECTO
ANNS  DOA   PHIL
IGOTYOUBABE
RAIN       SVU
YET   NNE   ARPEL
SLOB  APP   NINE
LINEN AID   ZOE
   LBJ    CHAZ
NICOLASCAGE
TREE  LAS   OPEN
LIEV  INS   RIND
CODE  EGO   NETS
```

Page 36: Amy Schumer

```
JOAN  GOT   HONE
ONTO  ANI   AROD
NEAR  RON   DEED
    EAT   NELLY
AMYSCHUMER
RAITT SAW   ABC
IMP   SHY   GRO
AAS   FOE   ISAID
DONRICKLES
MAJOR      LEA
ARON  IKE   GIRL
REIN  DEF   GREY
KANE  ANT   SADE
```

Page 37: Anderson Cooper

```
ABC   POR   HEY
BLAH  EWE   DANA
USNA  ANDERSON
COOPER     FLA
    MOL   OSWALT
LOGAN TRA   FIR
ARON  SID   CAVE
NAG   MPS   DEREK
GLORIA     ANN
   ORR    BATMAN
JEOPARDY   ROSE
ELIE  ODS   ALID
TIL   WES   LEN
```

Page 38: Padma Lakshmi

```
BLAH  SID   HOSS
RENO  ADO   IOWA
RANT  JON   ROAR
PADMALAKSHMI
   OAK    HOC
JUDGE RUSHDIE
UNI   GEE   AFT
TOPCHEF    INDIA
   OUR    EMO
WOLFGANGPUCK
ASIF  LEG   GAIL
FLOE  DRE   ANNE
TONE  ODD   TEDS
```

Page 40: Lady Gaga

```
   SAP   BAD    SEA
ANNE  ERR   JUST
LADYGAGA    ONCE
SPITE      OMAR
   ONE    ARETHA
BENNETT    CLOUD
OLE        AIR  NRA
SMACK  SINCITY
HORROR     BOA
   EPIC    ORBIT
FACE  DOWNTOWN
ERIK  ERE   ERAS
WED   RYE   RNS
```

Page 41: Chris Rock

```
JADA  HEAR  OPT
ACED  ELMO  MAO
CHRISROCK   ASS
KENNY      EARTH
   ANN    HRS
TOP   EATA  WIFE
HEAD  NOT   ENOS
ERLE  NOEL  COP
   AMY    SEA
ALANA      IDIOT
LIL   JANEFONDA
EVA   OTIS  ROAR
CEN   RAPT  ENYA
```

Page 42: Idris Elba

```
AOK   AHAB  LET
CLAW  TALE  ERR
IDRISELBA   TIE
DELLA      ASHOCK
   DID    STU
FREEDOM    SHESA
BIG   NEW   PIG
INOUR  THEWIRE
   RHO    ONO
LADIES     ULCER
ENO   THEOFFICE
ADO   TELL  ETRE
RIM   SAFE  YUL
```

Page 43: Victoria Beckham

```
ARE   LAMP  SON
HARE  EDIE  PUB
ACID  VICTORIA
BECKHAM     ELI
   OUR    FRENCH
SPICE KOS   GOO
TACH  SEX   MEOW
ORE   AOL   GIRLS
PACERS     AID
   RAT    ENGLAND
AMERICAN    EPEE
TEA   SISI  REAL
ELM   TATE  SRI
```

Page 44: Will Ferrell

```
MAN   GUYS  SHEP
ELO   ANUT  HEAR
DON   LILA  EERO
WILLFERRELL
   LOY    SAN
RUDD       SKY  JEB
ALI   PEPYS ODE
MAD   AMY   LEON
   ELM    DOO
JIMMYFALLON
HOME  LAND  RAG
INAN  ONCE  ATE
MIND  USER  LET
```

PAGE 35

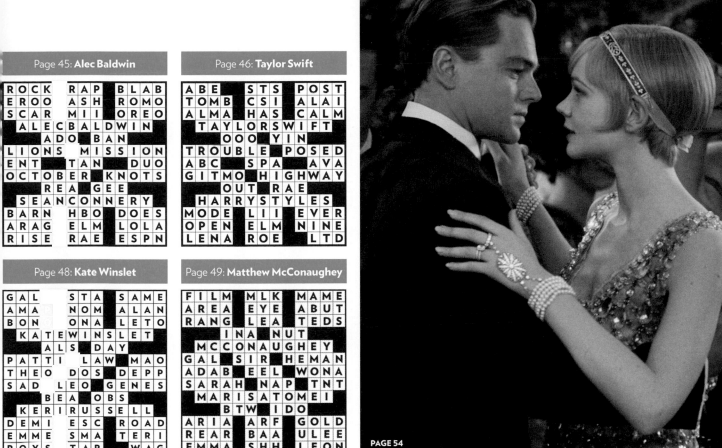

Page 45: Alec Baldwin

```
ROCK  RAP  BLAB
EROO  ASH  ROMO
SCAR  MII  OREO
ALECBALDWIN
   ADO  BAN
LIONS  MISSION
ENT   TAN   DUO
OCTOBER  KNOTS
   REA  GEE
SEANCONNERY
BARN  HBO  DOES
ARAG  ELM  LOLA
RISE  RAE  ESPN
```

Page 46: Taylor Swift

```
ABE   STS   POST
TOMB  CSI   ALAI
ALMA  HAS   CALM
 TAYLORSWIFT
   OOO   YIN
TROUBLE  POSED
ABC   SPA   AVA
GITMO  HIGHWAY
   OUT  RAE
 HARRYSTYLES
MODE  LII   EVER
OPEN  ELM   NINE
LENA  ROE   LTD
```

Page 48: Kate Winslet

```
GAL    STA   SAME
AMA    NOM   ALAN
BON    ONA   LETO
 KATEWINSLET
   ALS  DAY
PATTI  LAW   MAO
THEO  DOS   DEPP
SAD  LEO   GENES
   BEA  OBS
 KERIRUSSELL
DEMI   ESC   ROAD
EMME   SMA   TERI
ROYS   TAR   WAG
```

Page 49: Matthew McConaughey

```
FILM   MLK   MAME
AREA   EYE   ABUT
RANG   LEA   TEDS
   INA  NUT
MCCONAUGHEY
GAL   SIR   HEMAN
ADAB  EEL   WONA
SARAH  NAP   TNT
 MARISATOMEI
   BTW  IDO
ARIA   ARF   GOLD
REAR   BAA   ULEE
EMMA   SHH   LEON
```

Page 50: Beyoncé

```
BOB   PLAN   JIM
AND   RARE  TARA
RCA   INTO  HYMN
BEYONCE  LIZAS
   ICE  FIN
ADELE  HOUSTON
DID   OER   ARA
DESTINY  SORRY
   OVA  TEN
HORNE  FREEDOM
OKA   BEAT  EDA
LIV   EACH  AIR
DEE   TREE  REY
```

Page 51: Brie Larson

```
CANT   AMY   PAST
ALOU   NEE   ETTA
BARR   ITS   ROAR
  NAT   DONNA
BRIELARSON
LARRY  EIN   LAM
ARI   CBS   INA
HES  THE  CHETS
  VIOLADAVIS
JANIS  GER
USED  DEN   MARK
MILA  AGE   ODIE
PALL  NOW   NAVY
```

Page 52: Stephen Colbert

```
JONG   ATM   JRR
OBIE  SHOW  OOO
NINO  HASH  ANS
  ROOT  INDIA
KNIGHT  ITA
RODEO  STEPHEN
ONO   AGO   ELO
COLBERT  CHILI
  ABE  CAESAR
CARDS  DANA
IRA  EDEN  RAMI
TIC  NEED  SHIA
YAY  SPY   EARN
```

Page 53: Britney Spears

```
HURT   AMP   AFOR
ITAW   SAO   XRAY
NAZI  TRUELIFE
THEXFACTOR
   TRI   NOLTE
AFT  ARE   SOYA
BRITNEYSPEARS
BONO   EAR   NAT
AGENT   RED
   IGGYAZALEA
ORIGINAL  DEAD
LEAH   ALE   DIRE
DONT   WEE   YAPS
```

Page 54: Leonardo DiCaprio

```
IHAD   ACE   TRA
TARA  VAVA   OOP
SLIM  IRAS   MOE
 LEONARDO  HMS
  NET  ENYA
MUD  WOK  GENIE
OMAR  RAT  SKIN
MAYIM  LIN   SID
  LOAF  TAG
AWE  DICAPRIO
RAW  ALAN  ARFS
ELI  TERI  POOR
ALS   SEC   ENZO
```

Page 55: Pharrell Williams

```
TALE   ONO   SCAM
ASIA   WOW   COME
PHARRELL  OLIN
EER   ENA   MOD
   RLS  HAPPY
ENJOY  JOE   LED
LOUD  GET   PALE
SAL  OUT  GAYLE
HILLS  WIM
   AID  MAR  BET
PENN  WILLIAMS
ARNE  ENT   ALMA
LEAS  EDS   NEAR
```

Page 56: Matt Damon

```
KEEP   ADZE   MEN
ITSA   MOOR   IRA
MATTDAMON   LIP
   TEL   IRONS
JODIE  AREA
ALI   DANO  HAWK
IGO   STAUB  NIA
LAND  TITO   KIT
  AMYS  STAGE
DIANA   RCA
ROM  JONAHHILL
ENO  OXEN   ODIE
WES  ROAD   EADS
```

CROSSWORDS (continued)

PAGE 64

Page 57: Rihanna

```
PIES ONO WEST
IDLE DEF ASTA
TELL DDT LAIR
 SEED SHAKIRA
  NIA ENE
RIHANNA DREAM
USA  TIM  AGE
MADRE DOWNTON
 END LIE
DEMPSEY LENA
EVIL BOW SOLO
LANA RUE ONLY
ANDY ART NEIL
```

Page 58: Meryl Streep

```
GOES CRY  SHE
ARLO HEE SHED
DEER EDS HOLD
 MERYLSTREEP
  YOS OAR
DOA WES PRADA
MILA ANA IRON
CLINT ODD AMY
  GIA OUT
 ALECBALDWIN
ELAL ALL ANEW
LARS TEA ITTO
MIA  HER NOSE
```

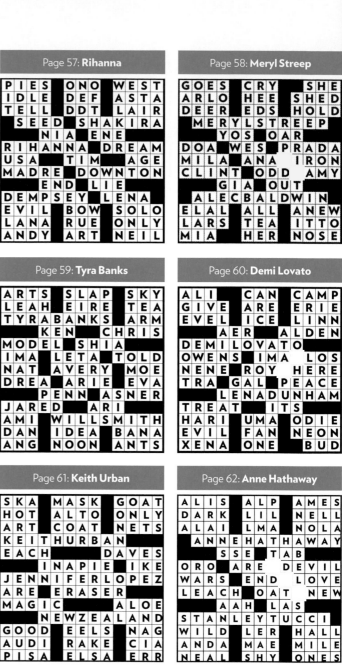

Page 59: Tyra Banks

```
ARTS SLAP SKY
LEAH EIRE TEA
TYRABANKS ARM
 KEN  CHRIS
MODEL SHIA
IMA LETA TOLD
NAT AVERY MOE
DREA ARIE EVA
 PENN ASNER
JARED ARI
AMI WILLSMITH
DAN IDEA BANA
ANG NOON ANTS
```

Page 60: Demi Lovato

```
ALIS CAN CAMP
GIVE ARE ERIE
EVEL ICE LINN
 AER ALDEN
DEMILOVATO
OWENS IMA LOS
NENE ROY HERE
TRA GAL PEACE
 LENADUNHAM
TREAT ITS
HARI UMA ODIE
EVIL FAN NEON
XENA ONE BUD
```

Page 61: Keith Urban

```
SKA MASK GOAT
HOT ALTO ONLY
ART COAT NETS
KEITHURBAN
EACH  DAVES
 INAPIE IKE
JENNIFERLOPEZ
ARE ERASER
MAGIC  ALOE
 NEWZEALAND
GOOD EELS NAG
AUDI RAKE CIA
PISA ELSA ERR
```

Page 62: Anne Hathaway

```
ALIS ALP AMES
DARK LIL NELL
ALAI LMA NOLA
 ANNEHATHAWAY
  SSE TAB
ORO ARE DEVIL
WARS END LOVE
LEACH OAT NEW
 AAH LAS
STANLEYTUCCI
WILD LER HALL
ANDA MAE MILE
NEAL SHY ONES
```

Page 63: Lupita Nyong'o

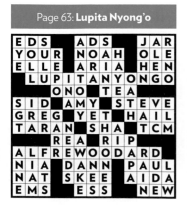

```
EDS ADS JAR
YOUR NOAH OLE
ELLE ARIA HEN
 LUPITANYONGO
 ONO TEA
SID AMY STEVE
GREG YET HAIL
TARAN SHA TCM
 REA RIP
ALFREWOODARD
NIA DANN PAUL
NAT SKEE AIDA
EMS ESS NEW
```

Page 64: Tom Cruise

```
ALAN AMIN JOB
PERI GINO ABE
TOMCRUISE CON
 KEN  NAKED
TEASE JADA
WAR SEAL HEAD
IVE ERNIE DRU
NEAR REED GOD
 LAST IRENE
BEAST LEI
ALL EMMASTONE
NIL AEON ANEW
DAY MADE SADE
```

Page 65: Jay-Z

```
JAYZ ARK ATEM
OREO ROI LOVE
BEAM INN INIT
 BUS GRAIL
EMPIRE DES
LOREN JOY IAM
ANAS BAM BALE
LAM MEG SUGAR
 BOY THRONE
HELLO RUN
TARA NRA ILIE
ERIC CID NEVE
DINK ENE GAYE
```

Page 128: Brad Pitt

```
ABS DEMI SAGS
BAT EDEN ERLE
BRADPITT VIEW
ARNETT OCEANS
 VHS TIN
SARI AAA PSY
THELMA&LOUISE
YAY ALE NEWT
 BRR LOG
TWELVE APEMAN
HODA ANNERICE
ERIC DEER RIM
MEEK YODA ADO
```

WORD SEARCH

Page 70: LeBron James
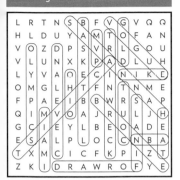

Page 71: Reese Witherspoon

Page 72: George Clooney
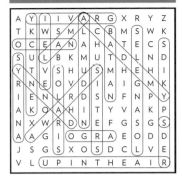

Page 73: Donald Glover
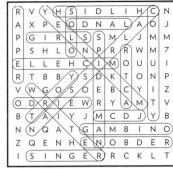

Page 74: Jerry Seinfeld

Page 75: Oprah Winfrey
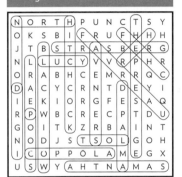

Page 76: Scarlett Johansson

ARROW-WORD

Page 80: Denzel Washington

F		D		G			A	C	
P	E	L	I	C	A	N	S	Y	R	U	P
U		O		M	I	K	E	I	S	E
D	E	N	Z	E	L		C	A	M	E	L
		M							S		H
F	A	M	E				H	O	D	A
M	A	Y	E				N	A	M
E		E						N	
A	R	E					O	R	A	L
I	R	K			S			O		E
C	R	I	M	E		T	A	C	O	M	A
A		W	A	S	H	I	N	G	T	O	N
I	N	S	I	D	E		R	A	I	S	I	N

Page 81: Heidi Klum

Page 82: J. K. Rowling

Page 83: Angela Bassett

Page 84: Tom Brady

PAGE 71

ANSWERS **123**

ANSWERS

CRISS-CROSS

Page 90: Ellen DeGeneres

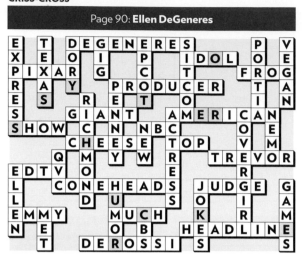

BONUS ANSWER: **OYSTER SHUCKER**

Page 91: Justin Bieber

BONUS ANSWER: **BRITNEY SPEARS**

Page 92: Kim Kardashian

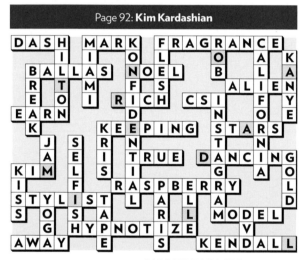

BONUS ANSWER: **ON A TREADMILL**

Page 94: Anthony Hopkins

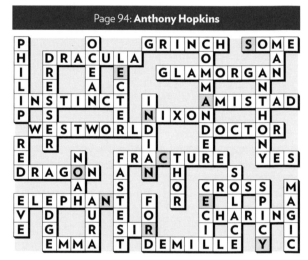

BONUS ANSWER: **SEAN CONNERY**

PAGE 92

Page 95: Viola Davis

BONUS ANSWER: **GEORGE CLOONEY**

WHODOKU

O	T	N	R	A	S	H	E	P
H	R	E	O	P	N	T	A	S
A	S	P	T	E	H	O	R	N
R	E	H	P	T	A	S	N	O
P	N	S	E	H	O	R	T	A
T	A	O	S	N	R	P	H	E
S	H	A	N	R	P	E	O	T
N	O	T	H	S	E	A	P	R
E	P	R	A	O	T	N	S	H

FUN FACT: **THE SOPRANOS**

A	S	D	N	O	T	E	R	G
N	R	E	A	G	S	O	D	T
T	G	O	D	R	E	A	S	N
O	N	A	S	D	G	R	T	E
S	E	R	T	A	O	N	G	D
D	T	G	R	E	N	S	O	A
R	D	S	E	T	A	G	N	O
G	A	T	O	N	R	D	E	S
E	O	N	G	S	D	T	A	R

FUN FACT: **DOG TREATS**

D	O	N	I	G	E	M	R	L
R	E	M	L	O	D	G	I	N
L	G	I	R	M	N	O	D	E
E	L	O	G	N	I	D	M	R
N	M	R	D	L	O	I	E	G
I	D	G	M	E	R	L	N	O
G	R	L	E	I	M	N	O	D
M	N	E	O	D	G	R	L	I
O	I	D	N	R	L	E	G	M

FUN FACT: **MODELING**

ACROSTIC

I	N		P	R	E	P	A	R	A	T	I	O	N		F	O	R
H	I	S		W	O	L	V	E	R	I	N	E		R	O	L	E,
H	E		S	T	U	D	I	E	D		W	O	L	V	E	S,
T	H	I	N	K	I	N	G		T	H	E	Y		W	E	R	E
T	H	E		S	A	M	E		A	N	I	M	A	L

A: AUSTRALIA B: MINION C: HELSING
D: REINDEER E: TELEVISION F: HOME G: HAPPY FEET
H: WHO I: WRINKLED J: STEWART K: HOVERS

T	H	E	R	E'S		A		M	A	N	N	E	Q	U	I	N
	I	N		R	Y	A	N		R	E	Y	N	O	L	D	S'
B	A	S	E	M	E	N	T		W	E	A	R	I	N	G		A
D	E	A	D	P	O	O	L		S	U	I	T		T	H	A	T
S	C	A	R	E	S		H	I	S		K	I	D	S

A: CANADIAN B: WISHES C: TURBO D: HIKE
E: LAMPOON'S F: DAISIES G: GREEN LANTERN
H: MYSTERY I: SANDRA J: HEAT K: SQUINTED

W	H	I	L	E		S	T	U	D	Y	I	N	G		A	T
B	O	S	T	O	N		C	O	L	L	E	G	E,		A	M	Y
	W	A	S		I	N		A	N		I	M	P	R	O	V
G	R	O	U	P		K	N	O	W	N		A	S		M	Y
M	O	T	H	E	R'S		F	L	E	A	B	A	G

A: RECREATION B: PHANTOM C: SATURDAY
D: GLUMLY E: GLOBES F: TINA FEY G: VENOM
H: SIMPSONS I: GOWN J: BIGALOW K: HAWK

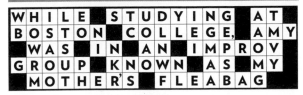

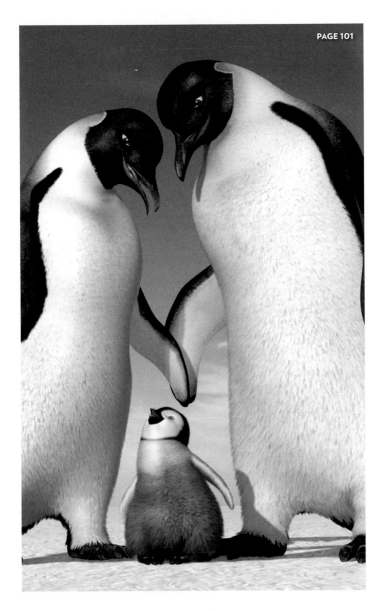

Page 106: Royal Role Model
1. The bystander behind and to the left of Prince Harry is no longer wearing his name tag. 2. Prince Harry's shirt is more buttoned up. 3. The yellow ball is larger. 4. The name tag worn by the woman behind Prince Harry has been shifted more to the right. 5. The capris worn by the woman behind Prince Harry have a longer hem. 6. The boy in the white shirt, right, now has a black sole on his shoe. 7. An additional cone has been added to the right of Prince Harry. 8. The upside-down cone behind Prince Harry is now right-side up. 9. The orange cone is now yellow. 10. The boy's shirt, far left, is longer.

Page 107: Seeing Double
1. The end of the letter "S" in the word "Sync" is longer. 2. A light bar among the row of lights is dimmer. 3. The red flag, center, is larger. 4. One of the vertical spokes in the window behind Beyoncé has been removed. 5. The dancer at far right is now wearing a longer glove. 6. The cape of the dancer at far right is now darker. 7. The second dancer to Beyoncé's right is now wearing a one-piece. 8. An audience member's wristband (second hand from left) is missing. 9. Tatum's belt is thinner. 10. The vertical gold band worn by Tatum has shifted.

Page 108: Healthy Hangout
1. The light behind Flay has been turned off. 2. Grenier is now holding even more beans. 3. Colicchio's right jacket sleeve is longer. 4. Another horizontal line has been added to Common's shirt pocket. 5. Common's shirt is longer. 6. The man's foot, bottom right, is no longer visible. 7. Common's shoe sole is black, not white. 8. One of the carrots held by Flay is shorter. 9. More tomatoes have been added to the basket behind Flay. 10. More bottles of Naked Juice have been added to the six-pack, left of Flay.

Page 109: Crowd-Pleaser
1. A flash has been added to a camera, top left. 2. Timberlake's album, held by a fan, has shifted slightly. 3. The navy cap worn by the fan behind Timberlake no longer has a logo. 4. Timberlake's pocket square is bigger. 5. The "A" on the fan's hat, right, is upside down. 6. The eyeglasses worn by the fan, far right, are now sunglasses. 7. Timberlake is no longer holding a Sharpie. 8. The top of the second "F" in "TIFF" is longer. 9. Timberlake's right jacket sleeve is longer. 10. The fan's phone case, far left, is now pink and white.

Page 110: A Very Popular Guy
1. The light-green stripe on the fabric behind Francis is now yellow. 2. A flash has been added to the camera. 3. The screen of the camera is now off. 4. The polka-dot tie on the man behind Francis is now striped. 5. The orange bracelet worn by the man, far right, is lower down on his arm. 6. The phone, bottom right, is larger. 7. The white phone's screen, bottom right, is brighter. 8. The jacket sleeve of the person holding the white phone is longer. 9. An additional button has been added to the man's jacket, bottom left. 10. The security guard's ear piece, top left, is now gone.

Page 111: Teenage Dream
1. The scrunchie on the girl, bottom right, is bigger. 2. The hat insignia on the girl standing front and center has moved to the right. 3. The brim on the hat on the girl left of Perry is lower. 4. The color of the phone right of Perry is yellow instead of pink. 5. A character in the center of Perry's shirt is gone. 6. There's an additional arm raised in the upper-left corner. 7. An arm to the right of Perry's hand now has a green bracelet. 8. Perry's earring is larger. 9. The white piping on the collar of the girl right of Perry is wider. 10. The sleeve on an arm over Perry's shoulder is longer.

Page 112: Rebel in Red
1. A dancer's diagonal chest strap is thinner. 2. The gold-and-black sword handle behind the backup dancer, left, is longer. 3. A second gold grommet appears on the backup dancer's hat, right. 4. The ring on a dancer's headpiece, far right, is bigger. 5. The middle gold stripe on the black helmet, far right, is gone. 6. A shadow of a hand holding a cell phone has been added. 7. Madonna's sash is longer. 8. The black portion of the belt on the backup dancer, left, is longer. 9. The row of lights, far left, has been extended. 10. A fourth gold stripe now appears on the backup dancer's helmet, left.

Page 113: Peace in the Kingdom
1. Chip's nose is pink, not black. 2. Chip's ears are farther apart. 3. Dale's left eyelid is more closed. 4. Dale's lighter-colored belly fur is smaller. 5. Strahan's shorts are longer. 6. Rock's crewneck shirt is now a V-neck. 7. The area where the sun is hitting the rocks at lower left is larger. 8. Strahan's left hand is no longer visible. 9. A pink flower has been added to the right of Dale. 10. The plants to the left of Rock are larger.

Page 114: Christmas Cuties
1. An additional light has been added to the orange circle behind Carey. 2. One of the red lights between Carey and the backup dancer is now orange. 3. The backup dancer's silver hat is slightly larger. 4. One of the red stripes on the backup dancer's shirt is thinner. 5. The red ribbon on the present is thicker. 6. A button has been added to Monroe's jacket. 7. A green light has been added to the cluster of lights between Monroe and Carey. 8. The stripe on Moroccan's shirt is gone. 9. Moroccan's Mickey Mouse sticker is rotated slightly counterclockwise. 10. Carey's necklace is longer.

Page 115: Jumping Jones
1. The gray shirt worn by the fan standing behind Jones is now a V-neck. 2. The wristband worn by the fan standing behind Jones is gone. 3. The rolled-up orange shirt, top right, is now yellow. 4. Jones's bracelet is closer to her wrist. 5. There is now more white fabric on the shoulder of the man sitting behind Jones. 6. The sleeve of the black shirt worn by the fan sitting behind Jones is longer. 7. The white paper cup, bottom left, is taller. 8. The "S" on the chair to the left of Jones is backward. 9. The "8" on Jones's chair is gone. 10. The type on the sign under Jones's chair is larger.

Page 116: America's First Dad
1. There is now a pen in the President's shirt pocket. 2. There is an extra red stripe in the American flag on the helicopter behind the First Family. 3. A backpack strap is also on Malia's left shoulder. 4. The helicopter vent behind Sasha is gone. 5. Michelle's dress is more buttoned up. 6. Sasha's dress is longer now. 7. There is another helicopter wheel. 8. The sole of Malia's shoe is lighter. 9. The President's shadow is larger. 10. The President's right sleeve is farther down on his arm.

Page 117: Drumming Duchess
1. The top of Kate's drum is cleaner. 2. The swoosh on the polo worn by the boy on Kate's left is bigger. 3. On far left, the hand's thumb is now visible. 4. The stripes on the tie worn by the man in the back are inverted. 5. In the back, there is an extra yellow ornament on the right side of the pine cone. 6. A fuzzy yellow ornament was added to the sweater of the woman to Kate's left. 7. The star on the sweater is smaller. 8. The same woman's ring is now on her middle finger. 9. The red polo worn by the student in the back left is unbuttoned. 10. On Kate's right, the "U" on the sweatshirt is flipped.

FRONT COVER
(from left) Samir Hussein/WireImage; Rich Polk/Getty Images; Andrew H. Walker/Shutterstock; Kevin Mazur/Getty Images; Samir Hussein/WireImage

TITLE
(clockwise from top left) Clay Enos/Warner Bros.; Ron Tom/NBC/Getty Images; Touchstone; Craig Sjodin/ABC; Chuck Zlotnick/Universal; Murray Close/Lionsgate; Guy D'Alema/FX; Barry Wechter/Fox

CONTENTS
2 (from top) Disney; Peter Mountain/Warner Bros.

PUZZLER TV
4-5 Courtesy Game Show Network; (Remini) Gregg DeGuire/Getty Images

CROSSWORDS
8 Alberto Rodriguez/Getty Images; **9** Isa Foltin/WireImage; **10** David Fisher/Shutterstock; **11** Jim Spellman/WireImage; **12** Shutterstock; **13** Richard Shotwell/Invision/AP/Shutterstock; **14** Chris Haston/NBC/Getty Images; **15** Will Heath/NBC/Getty Images; **16** C. Flanigan/WireImage; **17** Lester Cohen/WireImage; **18** Michael Tran/FilmMagic; **19** Dan MacMedan/WireImage; **20** Jon Kopaloff/FilmMagic; **21** Jeffrey Mayer/WireImage; **22** David Crotty/Patrick McMullan/Getty Images; **23** Steve Granitz/WireImage; **24** Dia Dipasupil/Getty Images; **25** Kevin Tachman/Getty Images; **26** Imeh Akpanudosen/Getty Images; **27** Beth Dubber/NBC/Getty Images; **28** Albert L. Ortega/Getty Images; **29** Jason Merritt/Getty Images; **30** Joe Scarnici/Getty Images; **31** Broadimage/Shutterstock; **32** Dia Dipasupil/Getty Images; **33** Rich Fury/Invision/AP/Shutterstock; **34** Alain Benainous/Shutterstock; **35** Kevin Mazur/WireImage; **36** Jason LaVeris/FilmMagic; **37** Jim Spellman/WireImage; **38** John Salangsang/Invision/AP/Shutterstock; **39** Smallz & Raskind/Bravo/NBC/Getty Images; **40** Matt Cowan/Getty Images; **41** Monica Schipper/Getty Images; **42** Mike Marsland/WireImage; **43** Angela Weiss/AFP/Getty Images; **44** Dave Benett/WireImage; **45** GP Images/WireImage; **46** Brian Friedman/NBC/Getty Images; **47** John Shearer/AMA2019/Getty Images; **48** Angela Weiss/AFP/Getty Images; **49** Jason LaVeris/FilmMagic; **50** Kevin Mazur/Getty Images; **51** Joe Scarnici/Getty Images; **52** Frederick M. Brown/Getty Images; **53** Steve Jennings/WireImage; **54** John Shearer/Invision/AP/Shutterstock; **55** Monica Schipper/FilmMagic; **56** Chris Jackson/Getty Images; **57** Steve Granitz/WireImage; **58** Jordan Strauss/Invision/AP/Shutterstock; **59** Noel Vasquez/Getty Images; **60** Jordan Strauss/Invision/AP/Shutterstock; **61** Steve Granitz/Getty Images; **62** Araya Diaz/Getty Images; **63** Shutterstock; **64** Anthony Harvey/Getty Images; **65** Paul A. Hebert/Invision/AP/Shutterstock

TRIVIA
66 (1) Nicole Weingart/Bravo; (2) Craig Sugden/CBS/Getty Images; (5) Netflix; (6 a-d from left) Kevin Foley/Getty Images; Craig Sjodin/ABC/Getty Images (2); Edward Herrera/Getty Images; (7) George Kraychyk/Hulu; **67** (Ariana) Chris Pizzello/Invision/AP/ Shutterstock; (guys clockwise a-c) Gregory Pace/Shutterstock; Invision/AP/Shutterstock; Matt Baron/Shutterstock; Rebecca Cabage/Invision/AP/Shutterstock; (royals) Chris Jackson/Getty Images; (animals a-d from left) Tom Reichner/Shutterstock; David Rasmus/Shutterstock; TMart/Shutterstock; Osetrik/Shutterstock; (college) Jorge Salcedo/Shutterstock; (flags clockwise a-d) Globe Turner/Shutterstock; warunee singlee/Shutterstock; Lukasz Stefanski/Shutterstock; iStock/Getty Images; (couples a-d from left) Shutterstock; Nick Harvey/Shutterstock; Richard Shotwell/Shutterstock; Angela Weiss/AFP/Shutterstock

WORD SEARCH
70 Gary Gershoff/WireImage; **71** Jon Kopaloff/FilmMagic; **72** Kevin/Invision/AP/Shutterstock; **73** Andrew H. Walker; **74** Jamie McCarthy/NBC/Getty Images; **75** Anthony Harvey/Shutterstock; **76** Marvel Enterprises/Kobal/Shutterstock; **77** Broadimage/Shutterstock

ARROW-WORD
80 Chris Pizzello/Invision/AP/Shutterstock; **81** David Buchan/Shutterstock; **82** Dave Benett/WireImage; **83** Dominik Bindl/Getty Images; **84** Taylor Hill/WireImage; **85** Kevin Mazur/Getty Images

TRIVIA
86 (1) Jonny Cournoyer/Paramount; (4) A24 Films; (5 clockwise a-c) Erik Pendzich/Shutterstock; Invision/AP/Shutterstock; Broadimage/Shutterstock; MediaPunch/Shutterstock; (6)Matt Kennedy/Marvel; (9) Fox Searchlight; **87** (Johnson) Kevin Winter/Getty Images; (locations a-d from top) ventdusud/Shutterstock; tishomir/Shutterstock; MNStudio/Shutterstock; Zak Zeinert/Shutterstock; (Gadot) Richard Shotwell/Invision/AP/Shutterstock; (Bond girls a-d from left) James McCauley/Shutterstock;Stephane Cardinale/Corbis/Getty Images; David Fisher/Shutterstock; Gregory Pace/Shutterstock; (TV clockwise a-c) Paul Hebert/ABC; Helen Sloan/HBO; Nicole Weingart/Bravo; The Food Network; (Batman v Superman) Warner Bros.; (celeb BFFs a-d from left) Chris Pizzello/Invision/AP/Shutterstock; Matt Baron/Shutterstock; Willy Sanjuan/Invision/AP/Shutterstock; Rob Latour/Shutterstock

CRISS-CROSS
90 Alberto E. Rodriguez/Getty Images; **91** Kevin Mazur/Getty Images; **92** Stephen Lovekin/Shutterstock; **93** Kevin Mazur/Getty Images; **94** Gabriel Grams/FilmMagic; **95** MediaPunch/Shutterstock

WHODOKU
98 Dan Wooler/Shutterstock; **99** ACE Pictures/Shutterstock; **100** Samir Hussein/WireImage; **101** John Lamparski/GC Images; **102** Han Myun-Gu/WireImage; **103** Tara Ziemba/Getty Images

SECOND LOOK
106 Alamy/WENN (2); **107** Spike (2); **108** Jim Spellman/WireImage (2); **109** GP Images/WireImage (2); **110** IPA/INSTARimages/StarTraks (2); **111** Alex Coppel/Newspix (2); **112** ChinaFotoPress/Getty Images (2); **113** Ryan Wendler/Getty Images (2); **114** Fern/Splash News (2); **115** James Devaney/Getty Images (2); **116** Jacquelyn Martin/AP/Shutterstock (2); **117** Chris Jackson/WPA/Getty Images (2)

ANSWER KEY
118 Chuck Zlotnick/Marvel; **119** Hilary Bronwyn Gayle/STX; **120** Moviestore/Shutterstock; **121** Warner Bros.; **121** Kevin Mazur/Getty Images; **122** Murray Close/Getty Images; **123** Tracy Bennett/MGM; **124** Brian Bowen Smith/E!; **125** Warner Bros.; **128** Tim P. Whitby/Getty Images

BACK COVER
Fern/Splash News (2)

meredith   MPA THE ASSOCIATION OF MAGAZINE MEDIA

Copyright ©2020, 2021 Meredith Corporation
225 Liberty Street • New York, NY 10281

15 ACROSS

Blue-Eyed Icon

&

ACROSS

1 "Six-pack" muscles
4 "Confident" singer Lovato
8 Droops
12 Word before cave, for Bruce Wayne
13 *East of* ___
14 ___ Stanley Gardner
15 *Moneyball* and *Troy* star (2 wds.)
17 *The* ___ (show for Whoopi and Joy)
18 Will ___ of *30 Rock*
19 First word of three movie titles for 15 Across (set in Vegas)
21 Pre-DVD format
22 Oz woodsman's skin
23 Bollywood actress's attire
26 Remote-control battery
27 "Gangnam Style" rapper
30 Sarandon-Davis road film that launched 15 Across's career
34 "Yippee!"

35 Quaff for Robin's Merry Men
36 Politician Gingrich
37 Shiverer's sound
38 "Captain's ___, stardate…" (*Star Trek* voice-over)
40 Number that's in three movie titles for 15 Across
43 Tarzan, for one
47 Kotb of morning TV
48 Author of *Interview with the Vampire*, the movie version of which costarred 15 Across (2 wds.)
50 Stonestreet of *Modern Family*
51 *The* ___ *Hunter*
52 Basketball-net holder
53 Earth's inheritors, it's said
54 *Star Wars* Jedi with three-fingered hands and large pointy ears
55 Hubbub, in a Shakespeare title Anika ___ Rose

DOWN

1 *Mamma Mia!* band
2 Actress-comedian Roseanne ___
3 Lee who created *Spider-Man* and the *Hulk*
4 20,000 leagues, as in *20,000 Leagues Under the Sea*
5 Shortens a film
6 New York baseballer
7 Counting everything (2 wds.)
8 Number that's in three movie titles for 15 Across (all by itself, in one title)
9 Diva's solo
10 "Rhinestone Cowboy" singer Campbell
11 Makes garments
16 *The* ___ *Wears Prada*
20 Goodbye, for Sophia Loren
23 Pig pen
24 "So that's it!"
25 Daisy Ridley's *Star Wars* role

26 *Duck Dynasty* network (2 ltrs.)
27 *American* ___
28 U-turn from NNE
29 "Are we there ___?"
31 Sportscaster Albert
32 Kelly Clarkson's "___ Gone"
33 Felix in *The Odd Couple*
37 *Meet Joe* ___ (15 Across movie)
38 Divided by painted lines, like a highway
39 *Phantom of the* ___
40 "Let ___ eat cake"
41 Disney's *The Computer* ___ *Tennis Shoes*
42 Falco of *The Sopranos*
44 Sorvino of *Mighty Aphrodite*
45 The alien's corrosive blood in *Alien*
46 *Finding* ___
49 Keanu Reeve's *Matrix* role

Answers on page 122